PANA CHOCOLATE

THE RECIPES

PANA CHOCOLATE

THE RECIPES

hardie grant books

From the beginning:
the Pana Chocolate story

Growing up in multicultural Melbourne, Pana Barbounis was fascinated by handmade things and artisanal crafts. He admired the focus and skill it took to make something from scratch, the patience it took to get it right, and the passion required to create something with love every time.

When a friend introduced him to raw handmade chocolate, he was hooked. He threw himself into research and experimentation, and discovered that chocolate could not only be healthy and all natural, it could be beautiful too.

After travelling to the UK and Belgium to work alongside traditional chocolatiers – the true masters – he returned to Melbourne inspired, with a vision to create a rich, luxurious chocolate that would set tastebuds dancing around the world.

For six months, he sequestered himself away in a commercial kitchen, trialling the recipes that would become the foundation for Pana Chocolate. He made raw chocolates in ice-cube and cake moulds, then hit the streets on his Vespa, taking the creations to trade shows, restaurants, family and friends – anyone who would try them.

He then started experimenting with pure essential oils, and developing unique new flavours. They weren't always a success – one lavender bar was especially disastrous – but through trial and error, he tweaked the recipes to perfection.

In the early days, he made, packaged and delivered all the orders himself. Before long, he had recruited a small team of talented wrappers and chefs, whose inventive approach to making raw chocolate led to delicious new innovations. Together, their goal was always to balance the hero ingredient – aromatic raw cacao – with flavours and textures that created a harmonious chocolate experience.

Pana founded Pana Chocolate in July 2012, building the brand around the notion of chocolate as an experience. He wanted to create a chocolate that made people stop, if only for a moment, to enjoy the myriad sensations it creates: cacao melting on the tongue, surprising bursts of citrus or herb, the character of coconut and a natural sweetness. He wanted to create a sophisticated chocolate that is at once smooth and textured, sweet and spicy.

The ingredients used in Pana Chocolate bars – and in the recipes throughout this book – are raw, organic and free from gluten, dairy, soy and refined sugar. But they are chock full of flavour, goodness and love, and are as wholesome as they are delicious.

The chocolate itself, handcrafted in Pana Chocolate's Richmond kitchen, comes straight from nature – think organic raw cacao, cold-pressed coconut oil and 100% pure essential oils.

As well as ingredients, ethics also matter at Pana Chocolate. This is why their base chocolate is certified Fairtrade, and is completely organic, kosher, halal, and vegan and vegetarian approved.

Pana Chocolate bars and recipes reflect Pana Barbounis's ethos: that food and love are what matter most in life.

WHY RAW?

Raw chocolate differs from commercial chocolate because it's unprocessed, and never heated above 42°C (108°F). Traditionally cacao was roasted when making chocolate, but today advanced processes such as cold-pressing mean the delicate flavour, nutrients and enzymes that are destroyed by heating can be retained. As with most plant foods, which are more nutrient-dense and easier to digest in their raw state, raw chocolate is packed with goodness.

It's high in magnesium, calcium, zinc and potassium, contains nearly four times the antioxidant content of processed dark chocolate, and is a natural mood, immunity and energy booster.

At Pana Chocolate, we keep it simple. Our chocolate contains only a handful of consciously sourced, natural ingredients They say less is more, but we say raw is more.

WHY ORGANIC?

All of our ingredients are certified organic because we believe they're better for you, and better for our planet. We're proud that our products, as well as our actions, contribute to a better earth. As of 2016, Pana Chocolate has paid for the planting of more than 34,000 trees, and we continue to pursue initiatives that support the environment.

We've fostered close relationships with our suppliers around the world, and because our ingredients come from across the globe – from Bolivia to Spain – we work hard to ensure our packaging supports local businesses. We partner with sustainable paper producers, and we use earth-friendly packaging.

What we're made of.

INGREDIENTS WE LOVE

Ingredients we love

All of the ingredients used in this book are raw, and free from dairy, soy, gluten and refined sugar. These are our favourite ingredients, and here's why we love them.

ACTIVATED BUCKWHEAT FLOUR

You can activate buckwheat by buying raw buckwheat, giving it a good wash and allowing it to soak for about 6 hours. Strain it and give it another good rinse. The buckwheat can become a little slimy, so place it on a non-stick dehydrator sheet and dehydrate overnight until completely dry.

To make the buckwheat flour, you need to grind the activated buckwheat until it resembles flour. Alternatively, you can buy activated buckwheat flour from health food shops. Then the work is already done.

It is important to use activated buckwheat flour when it is called for. This is because raw buckwheat and plain buckwheat flour are not as absorbent, so the texture of your finished product will vary greatly.

BAOBAB POWDER

Known as Africa's superfood, baobab powder comes from the tree's fruit pulp, which dehydrates naturally on the tree. Extremely high in vitamin C, baobab powder is also high in fibre, antioxidants, calcium, potassium, iron and magnesium.

BEETROOT POWDER

Beetroot powder is rich in antioxidants and contains iron, vitamin C, potassium, magnesium and folic acid. You can find it in health food shops or make your own from dehydryated beetroot.

CACAO NIBS

Flavourful and deliciously crunchy, cacao nibs are super versatile – you can snack on them, add them to smoothies or nut and fruit mixes, or use them in your cooking. Cacao nibs are not as sweet as chocolate, but they're packed with powerful nutrients, antioxidants and magnesium to give you a healthy energy boost.

CACAO POWDER

Cold-pressed, unrefined and chemical free, cacao powder is dense with antioxidants and is a great source of magnesium, vital for muscle and nerve function, regulating heart rhythm, blood pressure and blood sugar levels. It's rich and bitter, too, appealing to your dark side.

CASHEW MEAL

Cashew meal is fine in texture and rich and nutty in flavour – perfect for cakes. You can buy cashew meal, or you can make your own by blitzing raw cashews in a blender until they're coarse and crumbly.

COCONUT BUTTER

Coconut butter is the creamed white meat of organically grown coconuts. It has a rich, creamy flavour and, as nothing is added, retains all the nutrients found in coconut.

COCONUT NECTAR

Rich, complex and smooth in flavour, coconut nectar is naturally sweet, nutritionally rich and very low GI – a perfect healthy sweetener. It's produced from coconut palm blossoms.

COCONUT OIL

The medium-chain fatty acids in coconut oil reduce LDL (bad cholesterol) levels and increase HDL (good cholesterol) levels, as well as lowering the risk of heart disease. Coconut oil also contains lauric acid, which is antiviral, antibiotic and antifungal, offering amazing benefits for positive health. Its multiple uses make it the perfect item for any household.

COCONUT SUGAR

Coconut sugar is a natural sugar made from the sap of a coconut palm tree – not to be confused with palm sugar, which is made from a different type of palm tree. Coconut sugar has its own subtle sweetness, is low GI and contains several nutrients, including iron, zinc, calcium and potassium, as well as offering numerous other health benefits. While not technically raw, coconut sugar is a healthier alternative to a dry sweetener, and can add depth and balance to ingredients.

FLAX (LINSEED) MEAL

Flax (linseed) meal is the broken seed that remains after pressing flaxseeds to get flaxseed oil. It's extremely high in fibre and protein, and a rich source of lignans. Flax meal adds a unique and pleasant nutty flavour to foods.

GOJI BERRIES

These bright orange-red superfood gems are sweet, healthy and have been eaten for generations in the hope of living longer. They are high in antioxidants, as well as containing several minerals and super-high levels of vitamin C and A. Eat them by the handful or add them to your favourite dish – either way, they're delicious!

HIMALAYAN PINK SALT

This pure, mineral-rich salt from the Himalayas supplies and assists in the cellular absorption of minerals, balancing the body's pH and supporting the respiratory, circulatory and nervous systems.

LACUMA POWDER

Made from lacuma fruit that has been dried at low temperatures and then milled into a fine powder, lacuma powder has a subtle, sweet caramel flavour. It is an excellent source of carbohydrates, fibre, vitamins and minerals, making it a healthy choice for those seeking to decrease their sugar consumption.

LIGHT AGAVE NECTAR

High quality, all natural, raw and 100% organic, light agave nectar is produced with minimal processing and no chemicals, making it an excellent choice compared with refined sugars. A small amount of nectar provides a large amount of sweetness, which means a little goes a long way.

LIQUID SMOKE

Available from speciality gourmet grocers, liquid smoke can be used to create or enhance the smokiness of your dish. Liquid smoke can be used both in a recipe and on a finished product, and you can vary the smoke, from subtle through to intense.

NUT FLOUR

Nut flour is made from the wet pulp left over from nut milk, dehydrated overnight until completely dry and then blended in a food processor or ground in a spice grinder until super fine.

NUT MILK

A terrific vegan/non-dairy alternative, nut milk is rich, creamy and ridiculously easy to make using just filtered water and the nut of your choice (see page 184 for an easy-to-follow recipe). After extracting the milk you'll be left with pulp, which can be used in a variety of recipes, or ground to make nut flour.

NUT PULP

Once you've made your own nut milk you will be left with a nut pulp. This is a super useful ingredient for many raw recipes, and using it helps minimise food wastage. It is still quite healthy and fibre-rich, even after the milk has been removed.

RICE MALT SYRUP

Rice malt syrup is a versatile and natural sweetener made from organic brown rice. It has a rich flavour with a mild sweetness and is virtually fructose-free.

MAPLE SYRUP

A much-loved and well-known natural sweetener with important antioxidants and minerals like magnesium, calcium and zinc.

NUTRITIONAL YEAST

This vitamin-packed protein is low in sodium, cholesterol-free and a delicious, healthy addition to recipes and foods, especially salads, vegetables and vegan cheese (see pages 90–91). It's naturally rich in vitamins and minerals and can be found at most health food stores. A favourite among the Pana Chocolate team.

PANA CHOCOLATE BARS

Pana Chocolate bars are available from health food stores, greengrocers, independent supermarkets and department stores, as well as from various other great businesses around the world (visit www.panachocolate.com/stockists to find your closest stockist). Our bars can also be purchased online via our website.

If you are unable to find Pana Chocolate bars in your local area, substitute with any raw, vegan chocolate – but do check the ingredients, as not all are free from cane sugar, soy and gluten so your results may vary.

When melting Pana Chocolate for your recipes, be sure to stir the chocolate continuously until it reaches the desired thickness. This will ensure an even consistency and retain the integrity of all the ingredients.

PROBIOTIC CAPSULES

There are many health benefits to fermenting food – your gut will thank you for it, for one. In certain recipes we do this by adding a probiotic capsule, the same kind you find in chemists and health food stores. It's super easy and super good for you.

PUFFED MILLET

This gluten-free gem is the smallest of grains and has a mild flavour. It's a great ingredient for desserts and traditional, kid-friendly recipes (see pages 154–163).

PURE ESSENTIAL OIL

Great for adding flavour to your favourite foods, 100% pure and natural essential oils balance both body and mind. The oils are extracted through careful distillation and cold pressing – only the purest are used in our products.

RAW BUCKWHEAT

Despite its slightly deceptive name, buckwheat is not wheat, nor is it related to wheat. It is not a grain or a cereal. Rather, botanically speaking, it's a fruit seed. The triangular seeds are found in many raw food recipes, including cakes, crackers and granola, but they can also be used in more savoury dishes, as the taste is not very strong.

COCONUT MEAT

Coconut meat is the rich white lining that is contained within the shell of a coconut. High in fibre, coconut meat provides an abundance of minerals, vitamins and antioxidants, and is loaded with cholesterol-lowering lauric acid.

Note: This book uses a standard Australian 20 ml tablespoon and metric cup measurements, i.e. 250 ml for 1 cup. In the US a cup is 8 fl oz, just smaller, so American cooks should be generous in their cup measurements. In the UK a cup is 10 fl oz, so British cooks should be scant with their cup measurements.

Perfect your technique. Or just wing it. Your call.

EQUIPMENT AND TECHNIQUES

Equipment

Most of our recipes can be made using the basic utensils and equipment found in the average kitchen. However, here's a list of the main items that we use frequently. While these items will make life in the kitchen a little easier, don't worry if you don't have everything. We'll suggest alternatives where possible.

BAIN-MARIE/THERMOMETER

We use a bain-marie (also known as a double boiler) to heat and melt ingredients, as it works slowly. When used with a thermometer, this means you can ensure your ingredients don't overheat. The hot water is housed in the bain-marie and kept at a temperature required for raw food production. We then place a metal pan over the water, allowing us to melt ingredients or bring them up to the desired temperature.

If you don't have a bain-marie, don't worry. You can create a similar effect with a bowl sitting over another bowl of hot water.

To ensure your ingredients and recipes remain raw, the temperature of the mixture should never go over 42°C (108°F). This applies to all the recipes in this book.

CHOCOLATE MOULDS/CAKE FRAMES

These come in different materials, such as stainless steel, and give a professional finish to your cakes and chocolates. You can even use ice-cube moulds – that's how we started at Pana Chocolate while perfecting the flavour!

The right size cake frame can make life easy. It's a support for your cake and provides beautiful edges. Using a cake frame or the right size cake tin when portioning also helps minimise waste. If you don't have a cake frame at home, a square brownie tin will work just as well.

DEHYDRATOR

A food dehydrator uses a heat source and air flow to reduce the water content of foods. Removing moisture from food keeps various bacteria from growing and spoiling food. The dehydrator is usually set to 40°C (104°F), which means the food remains raw, and retains its nutritional content.

A dehydrator is a great way to achieve different textures for raw desserts. You can make biscuits and crackers, tart shells, etc. Although dehydrating is quite a slow process, given the low temperatures involved, this is a key piece of equipment if you're serious about raw food.

Dehydrating fruit for garnishes is also a great way to leave the fruit vibrant in colour, while making it suitable to garnish a cake for a cabinet.

Some recipes call for a standard mesh tray in the dehydrator, and some need a non-stick sheet. If you don't have a non-stick sheet, a sheet of baking paper will work, too.

Many of our recipes call for a mixture to be dehydrated overnight. It doesn't actually have to be night-time – just make sure you dehydrate for around 8–10 hours!

No dehydrator? No worries! Just turn your oven to the lowest temperature setting and place your mixture in the oven on a lined tray for approximately 1 hour. When using the oven, use the suggested times as a guide only, as each oven varies in its lowest temperature.

NUT MILK BAG

Nut milk bags are used when making your own nut milk, to strain the liquid from the pulp. If you don't have one at home, a piece of muslin (cheesecloth) will work just as well.

HIGH-POWERED FOOD PROCESSOR

High-powered food processors are used to make cake bases and nut butters, and for chopping nuts and more heavy-duty items. The food processor won't achieve a smooth result like a blender, but it will be your best friend if you're after a fine crumb.

HIGH-SPEED BLENDER

High-speed blenders are used to blend soaked nuts to achieve a smooth result. These are generally used for raw cakes, smoothies and liquid components.

UTENSILS

Rulers, spatulas, palette knives, paring knives and serrated knives are commonly used at Pana Chocolate, and they'll help you to get the finish you're after.

A ruler plays a key part in getting a perfectly portioned slice and ensuring a consistent product.

A spatula is used mainly for scraping things out of bowls and blenders. Its rubber surface ensures less waste, compared with using a metal or wooden spoon. A spatula is also good for folding in ingredients.

A palette knife (see 1, at right) can be used to scrape excess chocolate off a mould. It's also good for pushing down the base of a raw cake or getting an even surface when compacting a base, brownie or slice. A small palette knife can help lift something delicate onto a plate to avoid fingerprints and damages to the finish.

A paring knife (2) is good for slicing fruit, trimming the sides of a slice or cake and marking out garnishes on chocolate (for example, ruling a square or triangle shape). It's easy to handle and control.

A serrated knife (3) is great to cut cakes and slices. It's especially handy if you need to cut a cake that has chunks of nuts inside.

1   2   3

Techniques

The main thing to remember when making raw products is that blending or whisking some ingredients for too long may result in your mix 'splitting', and the oils separating from the mixture.

This can often happen with raw food because you are using a lot of fats (good, of course), such as cacao butter, coconut oil, nut milks and nut butters.

It is also very important to have your ingredients at roughly the same temperature. If you add a handful of frozen berries to a cake mixture that's at room temperature, your mix may seize and the oils will set, becoming lumpy and hard to blend.

This section explains techniques that will help you make the recipes in this book.

PIPING

There are many different piping methods, and each person will have their own preference. Keeping your piping consistent will help give your desserts a professional finish.

MAKING A PAPER PIPING BAG

1–2 Start with a completely square piece of baking paper. From approximately halfway up the square on the left-hand edge, cut a diagonal line down towards the lower right-hand corner of the paper, finishing just a few centimetres above the corner.

3   Fold the triangle's end corner towards the centre of the triangle, holding the squared-off end of the triangle in place.

4   Start turning your hand inwards, making a cone shape.

5–6 Adjust the tightness of your cone to form a neat, pointed tip on the end.

7   Bring the remaining paper up towards the top of the cone.

8   Tuck the edge of the paper into the cone, to secure it. (The square shape you made at this end of the triangle will help to keep it in place.)

9   Using a small ladle, pour mixture into the cone and pipe away.

1

2

3

4

5

6

7

8

9

WRITING WITH CHOCOLATE: TIPS

- Don't overfill your piping bag – about halfway is fine.
- Fold the end of the piping bag towards the opposite side of the seam.
- Hold the piping bag as you would a pen, and hold your other hand underneath, to keep everything steady.
- Keep your piping bag hole small – this will give you more control.
- If your chocolate is too thick, it won't pipe freely, so just add a little melted coconut oil (approximately 1 teaspoon) to thin it out.

- If you are writing a message and want to practise, lay a piece of baking paper over a written message and trace over the top.
- If you're not confident piping directly onto your cake or chocolate, pipe onto a plate or plaque.
- If piping on individual chocolates, line them up in a row so you can pipe from one to another without stopping.

RULING, PORTIONING AND SMOOTHING CAKES

Take the time to measure and portion your desserts with care. Smooth off the edges with a palette knife (see page 20) to give a clean edge. This will give the finished product a much more professional appearance.

MAKING INDIVIDUAL CHOCOLATES
LINING MOULDS

Note: *Ensure your chocolate mould is completely dry. Any little drops of water will leave watermarks on the finished chocolate.*

Melt chocolate slowly in a bain-marie. If the chocolate is not melting to a smooth consistency, you can add 1 teaspoon of coconut oil.

1   Hold the chocolate mould on a slight angle. With a ladle, spoon the chocolate over each mould to fill. Tap the edge of the mould with your ladle handle to release any air bubbles. This is especially important if your mould has lots of detail.

2   Tip the mould upside down over the bowl of chocolate and let the excess drip out, tapping gently with a metal spatula.

3   Run your spatula over the top and sides of the mould to remove all excess chocolate – this will ensure a clean and professional finish. Set in the fridge for 30 minutes.

Note: *Excess chocolate can be used to close off the chocolates once the fillings are in place (see page 26).*

1

2

3

FILLING AND CLOSING MOULDS

1   To fill the mould, place your filling in a piping bag. Squeeze some filling into each chocolate mould, leaving a gap of approximately 2 mm (1/10 in) at the top of each mould.

2   Ladle more melted chocolate over the mould to completely cover the filling and fill the mould.

3   Using a metal spatula, scrape off excess chocolate. Keep your hand and spatula flat to ensure you don't puncture your beautiful chocolates! Set in the fridge for at least 2 hours.

Note: *Once the chocolates are set, twist the mould slightly as you would an ice tray, then turn the mould upside down and tip the chocolates out.*

CHOOSING YOUR GARNISH

Don't clutter the cake. Think about textures and colours but, most importantly, flavours. Which flavours pair well together? Which don't? For example, you wouldn't use a peppermint garnish on a citrus cake, but blueberries and other fruit would be a match made in heaven. Don't go overboard with fresh herbs if they have a strong flavour. Try baby herbs instead – they're a lot milder.

All garnishes should be edible! We don't blame anyone who dives headfirst into a dessert, so everything on the cake should be safe to devour.

Try to leave a border or large area on the plate or cake free, with the main garnish only covering part of it. You've created something amazing; you don't want the garnish to steal the show!

1

2

3

FERMENTATION

Fermentation is a great way to change a food's make-up so it resembles a cooked product, while also breaking it down so it's easier to digest and creates a good bacteria balance in your gut. Examples of fermented food are sauerkraut and kimchi.

You can ferment by adding a probiotic; whether it be a probiotic capsule, or a fermented liquid called 'rejuvelac' (see page 185), which is made from sprouted grains or seeds left to ferment in filtered water until it becomes slightly fizzy.

FILTERED WATER

Many of the recipes in this book use water to soak and mix with. We always recommend using filtered water, as it's purer and cleaner than tap water. Substances in your tap water can affect the taste of ingredients; using filtered water means the dangerous contaminants have been removed and only the good stuff remains. It's also good to use natural spring water if you can find it.

HEAT SENSITIVITY

Raw foods can be more sensitive to heat compared with their baked or cooked relatives, and some components can melt easily. To achieve a great result when working with raw food, it's important to work in a room with a cool temperature and use cool utensils. For some recipes, we recommend pre-chilling your utensils in a freezer.

NUT MILK AND PULP

Making your own nut milks at home (see page 184) will mean you have a really fresh product, along with the added bonus of nut pulp, which can be used in several of our recipes.

SOAKING NUTS

Cashews and brazil nuts need to be soaked for a minimum of 30 minutes. Almonds need approximately 12 hours. Soaking gets rid of any dust or sediment on the nut, as well as making it quicker and easier to blend it to a smooth consistency. Once the nuts are soaked, you can remove them from the liquid and add them to your recipe.

Natural. Like your love of chocolate.

FILLED CHOCOLATES

CACAO CRUNCH

A chocolate filling for those who like a little crunch! The buckwheat adds a biscuit-like texture to the otherwise creamy raw chocolate. As well as being an easy and delicious chocolate centre for individual chocolates, this is perfect as an icing for raw desserts.

Makes: approximately 28 small chocolates
Time: 25 minutes preparation, plus 2 hours setting time
Equipment: high-speed blender, piping bag, chocolate moulds (or similar)

90 ml (3 fl oz) nut milk (see page 184, or use
   an unsweetened store-bought version)
100 g (3½ oz/⅔ cup) cashews, soaked
1 tablespoon cacao powder
60 ml (2 fl oz/¼ cup) rice malt syrup
activated buckwheat
2–3 45 g (1½ oz) bars of Pana Chocolate Raw Cacao

Place all ingredients except the buckwheat into a high-speed blender and blend until very smooth.

Transfer the mixture into a piping bag and pipe a small amount of filling into lined chocolate moulds.

Sprinkle some crunchy buckwheat on top of the chocolate filling, leaving enough space to fill the moulds.

Close the moulds with chocolate and set in the fridge for at least 2 hours. Once set, knock the chocolates out of the moulds.

Note: See pages 25–26 for step-by-step instructions on making individual chocolates.

CARDAMOM DREAM

A soft, fragrant filling for individual chocolates. Cardamom and chocolate are a unique combination, with cardamom adding a warm, spicy depth of flavour. Any leftover mix can be frozen for later use, or used as icing on raw desserts.

Makes: approximately 30 small chocolates

Time: 25 minutes preparation, plus 2 hours setting time

Equipment: high-speed blender, piping bag, chocolate moulds (or similar)

10 medjool dates, pitted

120 ml (4 fl oz) coconut cream

5 cardamom pods, seeds only

2½ tablespoons cacao powder

2–3 45 g (1½ oz) bars of Pana Chocolate Raw Cacao

Blend all ingredients into a high-speed blender until very smooth.

Transfer the blended mixture into a piping bag and pipe a small amount into each lined chocolate mould.

Close the moulds with chocolate and set in the fridge for at least 2 hours. Once set, knock the chocolates out of the moulds.

Note: *See pages 25–26 for step-by-step instructions on making individual chocolates.*

CINNAMON KISS

Our cinnamon kiss filling is sweet and woody, smooth and delicious, and the perfect accompaniment to a coffee on a chilly day. It's simple to make and is also a great topping for raw desserts and choc-brekkie granola (page 52).

Makes: approximately 35 small chocolates

Time: 25 minutes preparation, plus 2 hours setting time

Equipment: high-speed blender, piping bag, chocolate moulds (or similar)

230 g (8 oz) maple syrup

130 g (4½ oz) cashews, soaked

1 vanilla bean, split lengthways and seeds scraped

100 g (3½ oz) cacao butter

4 tablespoons ground cinnamon

2–3 45 g (1½ oz) bars of Pana Chocolate Raw Cacao

Blend all ingredients in a high-speed blender until smooth. Refrigerate the mixture in a covered container until it is firm enough to pipe into each lined chocolate mould.

Transfer the mixture into a piping bag and pipe a small amount into each lined chocolate mould.

Close the moulds with chocolate and set in the fridge for at least 2 hours. Once set, knock the chocolates out of the moulds.

Note: *See pages 25–26 for step-by-step instructions on making individual chocolates.*

FRUITY SPICE

As if you needed an excuse to celebrate the holiday season all year round – but here's one! This delightful filling is a nod to the traditional flavours of Christmas, combining the natural sweetness of dates and berries with the zing of spices. Simple to make, it's one to add to your favourites list.

Makes: approximately 35 small chocolates

Time: 25 minutes preparation, plus 2 hours setting time

Equipment: high-speed blender, chocolate moulds (or similar)

10 medjool dates, pitted and chopped

20 g (¾ oz) goji berries

50 g (1¾ oz) blueberries

3 tablespoons coconut sugar

120 ml (4 fl oz) fresh orange juice with pulp

1 tablespoon ground cinnamon

pinch of ground ginger

pinch of ground nutmeg

pinch of Himalayan pink salt

150 g (5½ oz) prunes, chopped into small pieces

2–3 45 g (1½ oz) bars of Pana Chocolate Raw Cacao

Soak the dates, goji berries, blueberries and coconut sugar in orange juice for at least 1 hour.

Gently blend the soaked mixture in a food processor until combined, being careful not to blend it to a paste.

Add the spices, salt and prunes to the food processor and blitz for 2–3 seconds.

Refrigerate the mixture until it is firm enough to spoon into a lined chocolate mould.

Transfer a small amount of the mixture into each lined chocolate mould.

Close the mould with chocolate and set. Once set, knock chocolates out of moulds.

Note: See pages 25–26 for step-by-step instructions on making individual chocolates.

GREEN GOODNESS

Matcha – or powdered Japanese tea leaf – is loaded with antioxidants and has a spectacular green colour and a delicate taste. You can find it in any good health food store. Blending matcha with lime for a fresh hit of citrus, our green goodness filling balances our rich, full-bodied chocolate for a taste sensation.

Makes: approximately 34 small chocolates

Time: 25 minutes preparation, plus 2 hours setting time

Equipment: high-speed blender, piping bag, chocolate moulds (or similar)

250 ml (8½ fl oz/1 cup) light agave nectar

130 g (4½ oz) cashews, soaked

100 g (3½ oz) cacao butter

1 vanilla bean, split lengthways and seeds scraped

4 drops lime essential oil

2 tablespoons matcha powder

2–3 45 g (1½ oz) bars of Pana Chocolate Raw Cacao

Blend the light agave nectar, cashews, cacao butter and vanilla seeds in a high-speed blender until smooth.

Add the lime essential oil and matcha powder to the mixture and blend until combined.

Refrigerate the mixture until it is firm enough to pipe into each lined chocolate mould.

Transfer the mixture into a piping bag and pipe a small amount into each lined chocolate mould.

Close the moulds with chocolate and set in the fridge for at least 2 hours. Once set, knock the chocolates out of the moulds.

Note: See pages 25–26 for step-by-step instructions on making individual chocolates.

MINI SNEAKERS

Yes, that's 'sneakers', not ... you know. A much-loved staple at the Pana Chocolate shops, our sneakers bar is a twist on the commercial favourite. This dreamy pairing of nuts, caramel and cacao is chock full of crunch and sweetness. We've used tahini to create a yummy, firm caramel and added some activated almonds for a textural crunch. The caramel is piped into individual chocolate moulds here, but you can also use it for the topping of any raw dessert.

Makes: approximately 14 small chocolates

Time: 20 minutes preparation, plus 2 hours setting time

Equipment: high-speed blender, bain-marie, tray

50 g (1¾ oz) tahini

4 medjool dates, pitted

1 tablespoon filtered water

1 tablespoon coconut nectar

50 g (1¾ oz) coconut butter

juice of ½ lemon

pinch of Himalayan pink salt

42 activated almond halves

3 × 45 g (1½ oz) bars of Pana Chocolate Raw Cacao, broken into pieces

Blend all ingredients except the nuts and chocolate in a high-speed blender until smooth.

Transfer the mixture to a bowl or tray and refrigerate to firm up a little.

Once firm, remove the mixture from the fridge and weigh out 50 g (1¾ oz) portions.

Roll each portion into a 20 cm (8 in) sausage.

Place 3 almond halves on top of the end of one sausage, then cut a slice at the end of the last almond placed. Repeat until all mixture and almonds have been used, then place the bars on a tray in the freezer to firm up a little.

Melt the chocolate over a bain-marie.

Using a fork, dip each bar into the chocolate, turning to completely coat, then tap off the excess chocolate and place onto a tray lined with baking paper. Repeat with all the bars, then transfer to the fridge for at least 2 hours to set further. Keep refrigerated until serving.

RASPBERRY RIPE

Berries and chocolate combine in this zesty chocolate. At Pana Chocolate, we love teaming tart fruit with our rich, raw chocolate, and these Raspberry Ripe bites get the balance just right. Using frozen raspberries, zingy orange zest for a hit of citrus and coconut for added texture, the mix is a winner for chocolate filling and as an accompaniment to your raw desserts.

Makes: 14 bites

Time: 25 minutes preparation, plus 2 hours setting time

Equipment: chocolate moulds (or similar)

50 ml (1¾ fl oz) coconut cream

3 teaspoons coconut oil

3 teaspoons rice malt syrup

45 g (1½ oz/½ cup) desiccated coconut

zest of ½ orange

20 g (¾ oz) frozen raspberries

2–3 45 g (1½ oz) bars of Pana Chocolate Raw Cacao

Combine all ingredients except the raspberries in a small bowl, and mix together thoroughly.

Crumble the raspberries over the mixture and fold through gently.

Spoon the mixture into lined chocolate moulds.

Close the moulds with chocolate, then set in the fridge for at least 2 hours. Once set, knock the chocolates out of the moulds.

Note: See pages 25–26 for step-by-step instructions on making individual chocolates.

If you would prefer to roll the mixture into balls, place it in the fridge to set a little first. Once the mixture is chilled, roll it into balls and place them in the freezer. Once frozen, drop the balls into melted chocolate and roll around to coat. Once coated, use a fork to pick up each ball. Tap the fork on the side of the bowl to remove excess chocolate. Place the balls on a tray lined with baking paper, then refrigerate until set.

SPICED CHOCOLATE CHAI

Nothing beats a good chai on a cool day, so we played around with our favourite organic spices until we perfected our very own spiced chocolate chai filling. It's like your favourite chai latte has been poured inside your favourite raw chocolate – a match made in heaven.

Makes: 35 small chocolates

Time: 25 minutes preparation, plus 2 hours setting time

Equipment: high-speed blender, piping bag, chocolate moulds (or similar)

230 g (8 oz) maple syrup

130 g (4½ oz) cashews, soaked

100 g (3½ oz) cacao butter

2 tablespoons cacao powder

2 drops ginger essential oil

1 drop clove essential oil

5 drops cinnamon essential oil

1 drop cardamom essential oil

2–3 45 g (1½ oz) bars of Pana Chocolate Raw Cacao

Blend the maple syrup, cashews, cacao butter and cacao powder in a high-speed blender until smooth.

Add all the essential oils to the mixture and blend until combined.

Refrigerate the mixture until it is firm enough to pipe into a lined chocolate mould.

Transfer the mixture into a piping bag and pipe a small amount into each lined chocolate mould.

Close the moulds with chocolate and set in the fridge for at least 2 hours. Once set, knock the chocolates out of the moulds.

Note: See pages 25–26 for step-by-step instructions on making individual chocolates.

Seven sweet reasons to get up in the morning.

CHIA PUDDING WITH A KICK

This is a unique, chocolatey chia pudding with a cayenne pepper kick. Blending the chia is what makes this recipe special – you end up with a gorgeous, velvety mousse texture, perfect for breakfast, fancy dinners or an after-dinner treat. If you'd prefer not to spice it up, just omit the cayenne pepper, or replace it with freshly grated ginger. But if you can handle the heat, it's a great metabolism kick-starter.

Makes: 4 puddings

Time: 2 hours soaking time, plus 5 minutes preparation and 1 hour setting time

Equipment: food processor or high-speed blender, 4 serving glasses

4 tablespoons chia seeds

250 ml (8½ fl oz/1 cup) coconut milk/nut milk (see page 184, or use store-bought)

6 medjool dates, pitted

2 tablespoons cacao powder

¼ teaspoon Himalayan pink salt

¼ teaspoon cayenne pepper

1 teaspoon ground cinnamon

chocolate shards (see page 183), to serve

dehydrated orange slices, to serve

Put the chia seeds into a bowl with the nut or coconut milk and stir to coat.

Cover and leave for 2 hours, to allow time for the chia seeds to soak up the liquid.

Once the chia seeds have finished soaking, put the chia and milk mixture into a high-speed blender.

Add the dates, cacao powder, salt, cayenne pepper and cinnamon and blend on high until nice and smooth.

Divide the mixture between four glasses, then place in the fridge for approximately 1 hour, or until set.

ASSEMBLY: Stick 1–2 chocolate shards into each chia pudding. You could also garnish with an extra dehydrated orange slice.

CHOC-BREKKIE GRANOLA

Granola is an essential breakfast staple (though we nibble on ours at all hours!), and so easy to make. Using our orange chocolate bar in this recipe gives your granola a zesty boost, and means you can get your chocolate hit at any time of day. Play around with tastes and textures – you can mix up the fruits and seeds for added variety.

For a nut-free alternative, substitute nut butter for tahini.

Makes: 250 g (9 oz)

Time: 20 minutes preparation, plus 8–12 hours drying time

Equipment: high-speed blender, coarse grater or zester, dehydrator

30 g (1 oz/¼ cup) sunflower kernels

40 g (1½ oz/¼ cup) sesame seeds

30 g (1 oz/¼ cup) pepitas (pumpkin seeds)

40 g (1½ oz/¼ cup) activated almonds

45 g (1¾ oz/¼ cup) activated buckwheat

15 g (½ oz/¼ cup) coconut chips

25 g (1 oz/¼ cup) cranberries

1 quantity date and nut butter (see page 184, and note at right)

3 squares of Pana Chocolate Orange

nut milk, to serve (see page 184, or use store-bought)

fresh fruit, to serve

Combine all dry ingredients in a bowl.

Add some date and nut butter and massage into dry mix. Keep adding butter until all the dry ingredients are coated.

Using a coarse grater or zester, grate the squares of chocolate into the mixture and stir through.

Transfer the mixture to a tray and dehydrate for 8–12 hours.

Once the mixture has been dehydrated, break it into small shards and store in airtight container until needed.

Serve with nut milk and fresh fruit.

Note: *To make date and nut butter, make one quantity of nut butter (see page 184), then add 4 medjool dates (pitted), 60 ml (2 fl oz/¼ cup) of filtered water, and 2 pinches of Himalayan salt. Blend all ingredients together until smooth.*

EVERYDAY PORRIDGE

Who says porridge is only for chilly days? Using buckwheat (don't be misled by the name – buckwheat is entirely gluten-free!), our porridge is perfect for every season, not just the winter chills. Make it special with mixed fruits, candied nuts and coconut yoghurt.

Serves: 3

Time: 6 hours soaking time, plus 5–10 minutes preparation

Equipment: food processor or high-speed blender, fine sieve, dehydrator

180 g (6½ oz/1 cup) raw buckwheat

125 ml (4 fl oz/½ cup) nut milk (see page 184, or use an unsweetened store-bought version)

1 ripe banana

1 tablespoon nut butter (see page 184, or use store-bought)

2 medjool dates, pitted

pinch of ground cinnamon

pinch of Himalayan pink salt

coconut yoghurt, to serve

berry compote (see page 182), to serve

pear chips (see page 184), to serve

candy nut shards (see page 182), to serve

Soak the raw buckwheat in filtered water for a minimum of 6 hours (it can be overnight).

Strain and thoroughly wash the buckwheat, then pulse in a food processor or high-speed blender to break it up.

Add all remaining ingredients and pulse the mixture together until nice and creamy.

Serve with coconut yoghurt, berry compote, pear chips and a candy nut shard.

Note: This porridge can be made a day or two in advance and refrigerated until serving.

NO-NUTS BREAKFAST BAR

When you're busy, it's easy to turn to sugar-laden convenience foods, or skip breakfast altogether. These nut-free breakfast bars tick all the boxes – they're rich in vitamins and minerals, and simple to make. They're perfect for school lunches, and you can make large batches and freeze them.

Makes: 8

Time: make at least 1 day in advance; allow 24 hours for dehydrating

Equipment: food processor, dehydrator with mesh tray

30 g (1 oz/⅓ cup) fine desiccated coconut

45 g (1½ oz) golden flax seeds (linseeds)

1 tablespoon black and white sesame seeds

1 teaspoon chia seeds

2 squares of Pana Chocolate Raw Cacao, chopped

pinch of Himalayan pink salt

pinch of ground cinnamon

4 medjool dates, pitted

115 ml (4 fl oz) coconut nectar

50 g (1¾ oz) tahini

10 g (¼ oz) coconut butter

45 g (1½ oz) bar of Pana Chocolate of your choice

Blitz the desiccated coconut in a food processer until very fine. Transfer the coconut to a bowl along with the golden flax seeds (linseeds), sesame seeds, chia seeds, squares of chocolate, salt and cinnamon. Combine, then set aside.

Blitz the dates, coconut nectar, tahini and coconut butter in the food processor until smooth.

Add the butter mixture to the dry ingredients and massage together using your fingertips.

Divide the mixture into eight portions. Shape each portion into a bar and place on a mesh dehydrator tray. Dehydrate at 40°C (104°F) for 24 hours.

Melt the chocolate bar and drizzle over the breakfast slices. Store in an airtight container in the pantry.

Note: The mixture does not need to be dehydrated, but this means you won't get the crispy outer crust. If you choose not to dehydrate your breakfast bars, store them in an airtight container in the fridge.

ON THE BEACH BREAKFAST
PANA COTTA

Light, summery and oh-so-tropical, this breakfast pana cotta will transport you to warmer climes. Just add tropical fruits to make the perfect dish for weekend brunch, or transform into an indulgent dessert with raw cacao powder and luscious mixed berries.

Serves: 5

Time: make at least 1 day in advance; allow 24 hours for dehydrating; 5 minutes preparation

Equipment: bain-marie, high-speed blender, 5 moulds or serving glasses, dehydrator

100 g (3½ oz/⅔ cup) cashews, soaked

50 g (1¾ oz) coconut meat

50 ml (1¾ fl oz) rice malt syrup

50 ml (1¾ fl oz) coconut water

zest of ½ lime

50 ml (1¾ fl oz) coconut oil (melted over a bain-marie)

mixed tropical fruit or berries, to serve

1 quantity coconut crumble (see page 183), to serve

baby herbs and/or edible flowers, to garnish

Blend the cashews, coconut meat, rice malt syrup, coconut water and lime zest in a high-speed blender until very smooth. Fold in the melted coconut oil.

Pour the mixture into the desired moulds or serving glasses. If you will be serving the pana cotta straight from the glasses, leave in the refrigerator for 2 hours or until set. If you are using a mould, set in the freezer for at least 4 hours (check that it's super firm) before unmoulding.

ASSEMBLY: Peel, cut and dice the chosen fruits. If unmoulding, place the pana cotta in the middle of a serving bowl or plate and scatter fruit and coconut crumble around it. If leaving in serving glasses, sprinkle the fruit and coconut crumble over the top. Garnish with baby herbs and/or edible flowers.

PANA CHOCOLATE CEREAL

Say farewell to boring cereal! A few dehydrator techniques come together in this recipe for a tasty, textural breakfast cereal. After all, who doesn't want chocolate for breakfast?
You can alternate the fruits to your taste, and make a big batch – the cereal keeps well in an airtight container. If you love it as much as we do, you'll probably find yourself snacking on it throughout the day, too! Keep it in a jar on your desk, pack a container for a post-gym pick-me-up or store in the pantry for a midnight treat.

Serves: 4–6

Time: make a big batch at least 1 day in advance; allow 24 hours for dehydrating

Equipment: dehydrator, non-stick sheet, food processor

candy nut shard (see page 182), broken into pieces

coconut crumble (see page 183)

dehydrated fruit

nut milk, to serve (see page 184, or use store-bought)

CHIA CRISP

6 tablespoons chia seeds

280 ml (9½ fl oz) filtered water

4 tablespoons cacao powder

4 tablespoons coconut sugar

To make the chia crisps, combine all the ingredients in a bowl and stir to coat the dry ingredients in the filtered water.
Cover the bowl and set aside for 2 hours, until the chia seeds swell and soak up the water.
Spread the mixture onto a non-stick sheet and dehydrate at 40°C (104°F) overnight.
Allow the mixture to cool, then break into shards.

ASSEMBLY: Toss together the candy nut shard, coconut crumble, dehydrated fruit and chia crisp. Store in an airtight container in a cool, dark place. To serve, add nut milk.

SUNNY SIDE SMOOTHIE BOWL

Start your day on the bright side with a vibrant, nutrient-dense smoothie so decadent you'll need to eat it with a spoon. You can create different flavours according to what's in season, and garnish with choc-brekkie granola or Pana Chocolate cereal (see pages 52 and 60) for your morning crunch.

Serves: 2

Time: 5 minutes preparation

Equipment: food processor or high-speed blender

120 ml (4 fl oz) nut milk (see page 184, or use store-bought)

135 g (5 oz) frozen banana

70 g (2½ oz) frozen blueberries

3 tablespoons coconut meat

pinch of Himalayan pink salt

pinch of ground cinnamon

Blend all the ingredients in a high-speed blender until smooth. Pour the smoothie into bowls and garnish with fresh fruit and granola or Pana Chocolate cereal (see page 60).

Note: *Be careful not to over-blend the mixture, or the smoothie ingredients will melt too much (although, if they do melt, you can just drink it through a straw!).*

A good dessert is hard to find (it's been here the whole time).

BISCOTTI BRÛLÉE

BISCOTTI BRÛLÉE

An easy crowd favourite, our brûlée combines smooth custard cream with hints of cardamom and a crisp pistachio biscotti. Tap through the biscuit to reach the cream, just as you would a traditional brûlée. It's the perfect sweet treat to serve with coffee at the end of a meal.

Serves: 3

Time: 10 minutes preparation, plus 2 hours setting and 12 hours dehydrating time

Equipment: blender, 3 serving glasses, cookie cutter (a little bigger than the diameter of the serving glass to allow for some shrinking), dehydrator with mesh tray

BISCOTTI

100 g (3½ oz) nut pulp (or use pulp left over from homemade nut milk)

2 tablespoons desiccated coconut

2 tablespoons coconut sugar

4 tablespoons fine pistachio meal

2 heaped tablespoons chopped pistachios

1 teaspoon matcha powder

Massage all the ingredients together until combined.

Roll out thin and flat between two pieces of baking paper.

Cut rounds big enough to cover the top of your serving glass, allowing a little extra for some shrinking.

Freeze the rounds to firm up a little – this will make handling them easier.

Place the rounds onto a mesh dehydrator tray and dehydrate at 40°C (104°F) for approximately 12 hours.

BRÛLÉE

130 g (4½ oz) cashews, soaked

90 ml (3 fl oz) coconut nectar

50 g (1¾ oz) coconut butter

20 ml (¾ fl oz) coconut oil

45 ml (1½ fl oz) coconut cream

3 cardamom pods, use seeds only

coconut sugar, for sprinkling

Blend all the ingredients except the coconut sugar in a high-speed blender until very smooth.

Divide the mixture among the serving glasses and place in the fridge to set for about 1 hour.

To serve, sprinkle the top with a little coconut sugar and rest a piece of biscotti on the rim of each glass.

BUTTERSCOTCH APPLE CRUMBLE

BUTTERSCOTCH APPLE CRUMBLE

With all the taste and texture of a traditional apple crumble, our recipe uses a whole marinated apple to make a gorgeous, comforting dessert. Perfect for cooler days or as an anytime treat, it looks impressive (so it's perfect for dinner parties) as well as tasting divine. The addition of a ginger crumble gives it a delicious, zesty tang while the butterscotch sauce adds sticky sweetness.

Makes: 1

Time: 35 minutes preparation, plus marinating and dehydrating time

Equipment: food processor, blender, dehydrator with mesh tray

1 quantity butterscotch sauce (see page 182)

1 quantity vanilla custard (see page 185)

1 quantity coconut ice cream (see page 184)

MARINATED APPLE

2 tablespoons lemon juice

20 ml (¾ fl oz) coconut nectar

1 vanilla bean, split lengthways and seeds scraped

pinch of ground cinnamon

240 ml (8 fl oz) filtered water

1 small apple, cut horizontally into 3 thick slices (with core removed, if desired)

Combine the lemon juice, coconut nectar, vanilla seeds, cinnamon and water in a container.

Submerge the apple slices in the liquid.

Place a paper cartouche (a piece of baking paper) over the top of the apple and weigh it down with a bowl or plate to ensure the apple slices remain completely submerged.

Place into the dehydrator at 40°C (104°F) for approximately 12 hours or until the apple is soft but still holding its shape.

Place the container into the fridge to cool.

APPLE CARAMEL

1 small apple, peeled, cored and roughly diced

80 ml (2½ fl oz) butterscotch sauce (see page 182)

Blitz the apple and butterscotch sauce in food processor until broken up and combined.

CRUMBLE

80 g (2¾ oz) activated buckwheat

120 g (4½ oz) nut butter

35 g (1¼ oz) coconut chips

4 tablespoons coconut sugar

juice of ½ orange

pinch of ground cinnamon

Blitz the activated buckwheat into food processor until slightly broken up.

Pour into a bowl and add the nut butter, coconut chips, coconut sugar and orange juice.

Massage the ingredients together and allow the mixture to clump.

Place the clumps of mixture on a mesh dehydrator tray and dehydrate at 40°C (104°F) for approximately 12 hours.

Allow to cool and then keep in an airtight container.

GINGER CRUMBLE

90 g (3 oz/1 cup) fine desiccated coconut

90 g (3 oz) nut flour

pinch of Himalayan pink salt

grated fresh ginger, to taste

zest of 1 lemon

90 ml (3 fl oz) coconut nectar

Blitz the coconut and flour together in a food processor until the mixture becomes super fine.

Pour into a bowl and add the salt, ginger and lemon zest.

Massage in the coconut nectar and allow the mixture to clump together.

Place on a mesh dehydrator tray and dehydrate at 40°C (104°F) for approximately 12 hours.

Allow to cool, then store in an airtight container until needed.

ASSEMBLY: Spread some butterscotch sauce on a plate. Place the base of the apple on the plate, then layer with some custard, apple caramel and crumbles. Place the second piece of apple on top and repeat. Finish by placing the remaining apple piece on top. Add a little crumble at one end of the plate and sit a quenelle of ice cream on top.

DECONSTRUCTED ETON MESS

Our take on this quintessential English classic teams crisp 'meringue', berries and vanilla custard for a raw, modern dessert. Traditionally served in a glass, we've deconstructed ours and added seasonal berries and fruit. Additional citrus or extra zest in the meringue will add a brightness, while freeze-dried fruit will enhance the texture. Garnish with baby herbs and edible flowers for a pretty finish.

Makes: 2

Time: 20 minutes preparation, plus 32 hours setting and dehydrating time

Equipment: blender, dehydrator, non-stick sheet, piping bag

fresh strawberries or other fruit, sliced

1 quantity vanilla custard (see page 185)

1 quantity raspberry jam (see page 184)

baby herbs, to garnish

edible flowers, to garnish

MERINGUE

50 ml (1¾ fl oz) coconut cream

2 teaspoons light agave nectar

3 tablespoons desiccated coconut

Refrigerate the coconut cream overnight. When ready to use, scoop the solid cream off the top, discarding the water left in the can.

To make the meringue, mix all the ingredients together in a bowl, then pour the mixture onto a non-stick sheet and dehydrate at 40°C (104°F) for 24 hours.

Every now and then, check the hydration of the meringue and flip it over. Once dehydrated, transfer to a mesh dehydrator tray to get more airflow and dry for a further 8 hours.

Allow to cool, then break into shards.

ASSEMBLY: Pile some fresh strawberries or other fresh fruit of your choosing on a plate along with some vanilla custard, raspberry jam, meringue shards and some freeze-dried strawberries. Garnish with fresh baby herbs and/or flowers if you have them.

RASPBERRY GINGER TRIFLE

RASPBERRY GINGER TRIFLE

The humble trifle, a Christmas favourite in many Australian households, is an easy dessert to create using raw, organic ingredients. Our ginger jam scroll adds a summery freshness that cuts through the creamy vanilla custard and sweet raspberry jam. Once you add some jelly and fresh, seasonal fruit, it's a winner, whatever the occasion.

Serves: 4

Time: 30 minutes preparation, plus 3 hours setting time

Equipment: food processor

1 quantity raspberry jam (see page 184)

1 quantity vanilla custard (see page 185)

seasonal fruit, sliced, to garnish

baby herbs, to garnish

GINGER JAM SCROLL

90 g (3 oz/1 cup) fine desiccated coconut

90 g (3 oz) nut flour

pinch of Himalayan pink salt

grated fresh ginger, to taste

zest of 1 lemon

90 ml (3 fl oz) coconut nectar

100 g (3½ oz/⅓ cup) raspberry jam (see page 184)

Blitz the coconut and nut flour together until the mixture becomes super fine. Pour the mixture into a bowl and mix in the salt, ginger and lemon zest.

Massage the coconut nectar into the mixture until all the ingredients are well combined.

Roll the mixture out between two sheets of baking paper until approximately 5 cm (2 in) thick.

Remove the top sheet of baking paper and spread the raspberry jam onto the mixture.

Using the bottom layer of baking paper to help you, roll the mixture up to form a jam cake roll.

Put on a tray and set in the fridge for approximately 15 minutes, then cut into 1 cm (½ in) thick slices when ready to assemble.

JELLIES

70 g (2½ oz) fruit purée (blended fruit)

1 tablespoon rice malt syrup

1 tablespoon psyllium husks

chilli, optional

Blend the fruit purée and rice malt syrup in a high-speed blender until smooth.

Pour the mixture into a bowl and stir the psyllium husks through.

Allow the mixture to sit until it thickens and becomes gelatinous. This should take about 10 minutes.

Transfer the mixture to a piping bag and pipe 16 dots the size of marbles onto a tray.

Set in the fridge for 10 minutes.

ASSEMBLY: Layer four slices of ginger jam scroll into a serving glass with 1 tablespoon of custard, 1 tablespoon of raspberry jam and four fruit jellies, and garnish with seasonal fruit and baby herbs.

STICKY DATE

This raw sticky date brownie is full of crunchy walnuts and smothered in a thickbutterscotch sauce. The refreshing coconut ice cream provides a little lightness and balance to this sweet and lavish dessert.

Serves: 4–6

Time: 25 minutes preparation, plus 12 hours dehydrating time

Equipment: food processor, 20 cm × 20 cm (8 in × 8 in) brownie or cake tin, dehydrator with mesh tray

1 quantity coconut ice cream (see page 184)

1 quantity butterscotch sauce (see page 182)

STICKY DATE BROWNIE

50 g (1¾ oz/½ cup) desiccated coconut

6½ medjool dates, pitted

50 ml (1¾ fl oz) filtered water

1 tablespoon lacuma powder

pinch of Himalayan pink salt

4 tablespoons nut flour

2 teaspoons cacao powder

25 g (1 oz/¼ cup) activated walnuts, roughly chopped

Line your cake or brownie tin with baking paper.

Blitz the desiccated coconut in a food processer until very fine, then set aside.

Pulse the dates, water, lacuma powder and salt in a food processor or high-speed blender, leaving the mixture slightly chunky. Transfer the mixture to a bowl and add the blitzed coconut, along with the nut flour and cacao powder. Massage together with your hands until all ingredients have been incorporated, then fold through the chopped nuts. Press the mixture into the tin to mould it into shape. Pop the mixture out of the tin and place it on a mesh dehydrator tray. Dehydrate overnight at 40°C (104°F).

Cut the brownie into four to six portions and serve with coconut ice cream and butterscotch sauce.

Dessert rules were made to be broken.

BANANA RAMBLE

BANANA RAMBLE

We love taking one hero ingredient and pairing it with our all-time favourite flavours and textures. This dreamy dessert teams banana with caramel and sesame, making it the perfect combination of crunchy and sweet.

Serves: 5

Time: 30 minutes preparation, plus 1–2 days marinating and 8–10 hours dehydrating time

Equipment: dehydrator with mesh tray, non-stick sheet, food processor or high-speed blender

TAHINI CARAMEL

11 medjool dates, pitted

85 ml (2 ¾ fl oz) filtered water

2 tablespoons lemon juice

2 tablespoons coconut sugar

80 g (2¾ oz) date paste

1½ tablespoons coconut butter, melted

1½ tablespoons tahini

2 pinches of Himalayan pink salt

To create a date paste, blend the medjool dates, filtered water and 1 tablespoon of the lemon juice in a high-speed blender until smooth. Pass through a fine sieve, if desired.

Whisk the lemon juice and coconut sugar in a bowl until the coconut sugar has dissolved. Add all the other ingredients and stir to combine. Refrigerate the caramel until needed.

SESAME SNAPS

2 tablespoons black sesame seeds

2 tablespoons white sesame seeds

1 teaspoon tahini

1 tablespoon maple syrup

Combine the sesame seeds, tahini and maple syrup in a bowl and mix together.

Using a palette knife, spread the mixture onto a non-stick sheet and dehydrate overnight at 40°C (104°F). Break the dehydrated sesame snaps into pieces.

CARAMEL BANANAS

5 bananas (1 for each plated dessert)

maple syrup – enough to coat bananas

juice of 3 lemons

3 vanilla beans, split lengthways and seeds scraped

Cut each banana into three different sized pieces, each slightly bigger than the last one.

Place the banana slices in a container with maple syrup, lemon juice and vanilla seeds and marinate for a day or two in the fridge.

Once marinated, strain the bananas and place them on a mesh dehydrator tray and dehydrate overnight at 40°C (104°F).

CHOCOLATE CAKE

90 g (3 oz/1 cup) desiccated coconut

4 medjool dates, pitted

60 ml (2 fl oz/¼ cup) chocolate syrup (see page 183, or use store-bought)

Blitz the coconut in a food processor or high-speed blender until extra fine, then pour into a bowl and set aside.

Blend the dates and chocolate syrup in a food processor or high-speed blender until smooth.

Pour the date mixture over the desiccated coconut and fold the mixture together until combined.

Spread the mixture onto a mesh dehydrator tray and dehydrate overnight at 40°C (104°F).

Break into pieces.

BANANA ICE CREAM

400 g (14 oz) frozen bananas, cut into pieces

juice of ½ lemon

maple syrup, optional

Blend the frozen bananas and lemon in a high-speed blender. If you'd like a little extra sweetness, add a sweetener such as maple syrup.

ASSEMBLY: Spread a little tahini caramel across each plate and arrange the sesame snaps, caramel banana pieces and chocolate cake over the caramel. Scoop a quenelle of the banana ice cream on top of each plate, then serve.

'CHEESE' TASTING PLATE

'CHEESE' TASTING PLATE

This vegan cheese tasting plate is the perfect course to serve between dinner and dessert, or to pair with a glass of wine over lunch. Combining multiple flavours and textures, this dish is proof that vegan cheese is just as delicious as the traditional kind! It's a real showstopper – no one can believe the flavour!

Serves: 8

Time: 1–1.5 hours preparation, plus fermenting, freezing and dehydrating time

Equipment: fine sieve, jar, cloth, high-speed blender or food processor, dehydrator, non-stick sheet, nut milk bag or similar, 2 metal rings

NUT CHEESE 1 & 2

155 g (5½ oz/1 cup) cashews, soaked

80 ml (2½ fl oz/⅓ cup) rejuvelac (see page 185)

2 tablespoons nutritional yeast

pinch of salt

squeeze of lemon juice

liquid smoke

Blend the cashews and ¼ cup rejuvelac in a food processor or high-speed blender until smooth.

Transfer the mixture to a bowl, then combine with the nutritional yeast, salt and lemon juice. Divide the mixture in half. Line a tray with baking paper and put the metal ring on top. Transfer half the mixture into the ring and smooth it out. Tap out any air bubbles, then place it in the freezer to firm up a little. Pop it out of the ring and dehydrate at 40°C (104°F) for 24 hours. This will add a slight crust around the outside, as well as helping the rejuvelac along in the fermenting process. After dehydrating, place the nut cheese in the fridge.

Cover the bowl containing the other half of the mixture with a cloth and set aside to ferment at room temperature overnight. Stir the crust into the fermented cheese, then add a drop of liquid smoke.

Place the mixture in the second metal ring and put it in the freezer to firm up slightly.

Pop the mixture out and place it in the fridge, ready for serving.

NUT CHEESE 3

155 g (5½ oz/1 cup) cashews, soaked

60 ml (2 fl oz/¼ cup) rejuvelac (see page 185)

1 probiotic capsule

Blend all ingredients in a food processor or high-speed blender until smooth.

Place a strainer over a bowl, then put a nut milk bag on top of the strainer and pour the mixture into the bag. Allow the liquid to strain through the bag and strainer into the bowl.

Cover with a cloth and leave the mixture to ferment at room temperature for at least 8–14 hours.

Scrape the cheese that has been created into a bowl and add the the desired flavouring. (See note below for ideas.)

Place the mixture in a metal ring, then leave it in the freezer to firm up before popping out.

Keep the cheese refrigerated until serving.

Note: You can add different flavours to your cheese, such as herbs or liquid smoke, or you could roll it in extra nutritional yeast, sesame seeds or peppercorns.

FLAX SEED CRACKERS

1 medium ripe tomato

3 sprigs of fresh thyme

pinch of Himalayan pink salt

1 tablespoon nutritional yeast

25 g (1 oz/¼ cup) mixed seeds (flax, chia, white/black sesame, buckwheat)

1 teaspoon flax (linseed) meal

Blend the tomato, thyme, salt and nutritional yeast in a food processor until smooth.

Pour the mixture into a small bowl and add the mixed seeds and flax (linseed) meal.

Leave the mixture in the fridge until the seeds and flax (linseed) meal soak up the liquid and the mix becomes spreadable.

Spread a thin layer onto a non-stick sheet and dehydrate at 40°C (104°F) for approximately 8 hours.

Break into shards and serve with cheese.

>

FRUIT BREAD

90 g (3 oz) brazil nut pulp

30 g (1 oz) flax (linseed) meal

4 dried apricots

4 activated walnuts

1 sprig of thyme

2 pinches of coconut sugar

2 pinches of Himalayan pink salt

Massage all the ingredients together.

Form the mixture into a small loaf shape and freeze to firm up.

Once the mixture has almost completely frozen, use a serrated knife to slice it into approximately 15 thin slices.

Lay the slices on a mesh dehydrator tray and dehydrate at 40°C (104°F) for 8–12 hours.

PICKLED VEGETABLES

310 ml (10½ fl oz/1¼ cups) apple-cider vinegar

185 ml (6 fl oz/¾ cup) filtered water

170 g (6 oz/¾ cup) coconut sugar

2 tablespoons Himalayan pink salt

1 teaspoon peppercorns

1 teaspoon mustard seeds

1 star anise

1 bunch of Dutch carrots

1 bunch of baby beetroot (beet)

To make the pickling liquid, place all the ingredients except the vegetables into a bowl and whisk until the coconut sugar has dissolved.

Cut the leaves off the carrots and beetroot. Using a paring knife, clean the carrots around the top and slightly scrape them to remove any dirt.

Place the carrots into a clean jar.

Clean the beetroot and cut them into small pieces, then add them to the same jar.

Fill the jar with the pickling liquid, making sure all the vegetables are completely covered.

Seal the jar with the lid, then store at room temperature for 3–4 days. Open the jar every day to release any pressure that might build up during fermentation.

After the fermenting stage, keep the jar in the fridge.

Note: To make a sweet pickling liquid, place fresh thyme in the jar along with the vegetables, then pour in 130 ml (4½ fl oz) maple syrup before adding the pickling liquid.

FIG PASTE

100 g (3½ oz) plump dried figs, diced

2½ medjool dates, pitted, diced

zest and juice of ½ orange

pinch of Himalayan pink salt

35 g (1¼ oz) beetroot (beet)

thyme, to taste

Blend all the ingredients in a food processor until fairly smooth (a couple of small chunks are fine).

ASSEMBLY: Arrange cheeses and accompanying items on a platter to serve.

COMING UP ROSES

COMING UP ROSES

Chocolate, raspberry and rose combine to create a luscious harmony of flavours. Here, they come together to make a rich dessert that looks as beautiful as it tastes. Don't be daunted by all the components. Just take it one step at a time – it will be worth the effort.

Makes: 5

Time: 40 minutes preparation, plus 2–3 hours setting and 8–10 hours dehydrating time

Equipment: fine sieve, bain-marie, high-speed blender, five 11 cm (4¼ in) metal rings, dehydrator, non-stick sheet, piping bag, 4 cm (1½ in) metal ring cutter

half a quantity chocolate syrup (see page 183)

baby herbs, to garnish

edibile flowers, to garnish

CHOCOLATE, RASPBERRY AND ROSE MOUSSE

100 g (3½ oz) raspberry purée, deseeded

45 g (1½ oz) bar of Pana Chocolate Rose, broken into pieces

1 teaspoon coconut oil

120 g (4½ oz) coconut butter, melted

100 g (3½ oz/⅔ cup) cashews, soaked

90 ml (3 fl oz) coconut water

90 g (3 oz) coconut sugar

2 tablespoons coconut nectar

To make the raspberry purée, blend the raspberries in a high-speed blender until smooth, then strain with a fine sieve to remove the seeds. Set aside.

Melt the chocolate and coconut oil together over a bain-marie.

Blend all the remaining ingredients in a food processor or high-speed blender until very smooth.

Add the chocolate mixture and blend until all ingredients are incorporated.

Pour the mixture into the five metal rings and set in the freezer. Keep frozen until needed.

BEET CHIA CRISP

2 tablespoons chia seeds

60 ml (2 fl oz/¼ cup) filtered water

1 teaspoon beetroot (beet) powder

2 teaspoons coconut sugar

1 teaspoon cacao powder

Mix all the ingredients in a bowl until all the chia seeds are coated with liquid.

Cover and leave at room temperature for approximately 30 minutes, or until the chia seeds have absorbed most of the liquid.

Spread (not too thin) onto a non-stick sheet and dehydrate overnight at 40°C (104°F).

Break into shards and store in an airtight container at room temperature until needed.

RASPBERRY GRANITA

60 g (2 oz) raspberry purée, deseeded

1 tablespoon coconut water

3 tablespoons coconut sugar

To make the raspberry purée, blend the raspberries in a high-speed blender until smooth, then strain with a fine sieve to remove the seeds. Set aside.

Whisk all the ingredients together until the coconut sugar dissolves, then freeze in a bowl.

After about 4 hours, or once the granita has frozen solid, scrape with a cold fork to break up the crystals.

Note: Place the granita on a frozen plate and keep frozen until ready to serve – it will melt quickly!

ASSEMBLY: Chill your serving plates and cutlery in the freezer or fridge. Use a 4 cm (1½ in) metal ring cutter to cut out the centre of the mousse (bonus – you can eat this for a snack!). Pop the mousse out of the metal ring and place it in the middle of a cold plate. Pipe dots of chocolate syrup and extra raspberry purée around the top of the mousse ring. Scatter a few shards of the beet chia crisp among the syrup and purée. Scrape the granita over the top of the mousse. Garnish with fresh baby herbs and edible flowers for a little extra colour and freshness, then serve immediately.

ORANGE GINGER ZINGER

This zesty dessert is bursting with ginger paired with creamy orange ice cream, resulting in a spectacular combination of raw dark chocolate and orange ganache that's not too rich or heavy. Using the dehydrator to make the ginger cake adds a unique texture to the otherwise soft raw components.

Serves: 3

Time: 30 minutes preparation, plus setting and dehydrating time

Equipment: food processor, fine grater or zester, dehydrator with mesh tray, 2–4 cm (¾–1½ in) cookie cutter, bain-marie

3 dehydrated orange slices

flesh of 1 orange, chopped

fresh orange, cut into chunks, to serve

fresh herbs, to garnish

CACAO SOIL

65 g (2¼ oz/¾ cup) desiccated coconut

60 g (2 oz/½ cup) cacao powder

5 medjool dates, pitted

pinch of Himalayan pink salt

2 tablespoons cacao nibs

Blitz all the ingredients except the cacao nibs in a food processor until the mixture comes together.

Add the cacao nibs, then blitz in a short burst, so the nibs are evenly distributed and slightly chopped.

Note: This makes ample cacao soil for the dessert. Any remaining mixture is perfect for garnishing coconut ice cream, or serving with granola, coconut yoghurt or chia puddings. Keeps well in an airtight container.

>

GINGER CAKE

1 flax egg (1 tablespoon flax (linseed) meal + 3 tablespoons
    filtered water)
90 g (3 oz) cashew meal
90 g (3 oz) coconut sugar
pinch of Himalayan pink salt
½ teaspoon grated fresh ginger

To make the flax egg, combine the flax (linseed) meal and water
into a small bowl.

Refrigerate for about 15 minutes. The water will be completely
absorbed by the flax (linseed) and a soft gel will form.

Blitz the cashew meal, coconut sugar and salt in a food
processor until very fine.

Transfer to a bowl and fold in the flax egg and fresh ginger.

Make sure all the ingredients are combined, but be careful not
to overmix.

Shape the dough to your desired thickness and then cut into
rounds with a cookie cutter.

Place the rounds on a mesh dehydrator tray and dehydrate at
40°C (104°F) for 24–48 hours.

Note: The longer you dry the mix, the more a crust will form on
the outside of the cakes.

GINGER SYRUP

3 tablespoons maple syrup
3 tablespoons filtered water
grated fresh ginger, to taste

Whisk all the ingredients together in a bowl, then store in the
fridge until needed.

Brush syrup onto the ginger cake before serving.

CHOCOLATE ORANGE GANACHE LOGS

1 quantity chocolate orange ganache (see chocolate
    ganache recipe, page 183, but prepare using a bar of
    Pana Chocolate Orange)

Scoop the set ganache mixture out onto a piece of baking
paper and roll it into a long log shape.

Return the log to the fridge to set once more.

Once set, cut the ganache log into nine pieces (three pieces
per serving).

ORANGE ICE CREAM

small handful of goji berries

135 ml (4½ fl oz) coconut water

160 g (5½ oz) cashews, soaked

150 g (5½ oz) fresh orange

65 g (2¼ oz) coconut meat

75 ml (2½ fl ozora) coconut oil

160 ml (5½ fl oz) light agave nectar

pinch of Himalayan pink salt

Soak the goji berries in coconut water for about 15 minutes. You don't need many gojis – the more berries the more intense the colour will be.

Once plump, blitz the berries and coconut water with all the remaining ingredients in a high-speed blender until very smooth. Pass the mixture through a fine sieve to ensure your ice cream is smooth and creamy.

Set in a shallow container in the freezer.

Once set, roughly chop the ice cream and blend it in a food processor until creamy.

Serve immediately.

Note: *If you re-freeze the ice cream after it has been blended for the second time, it may become quite hard. If this is the case, re-blend in a food processor before serving – it will return to that creamy texture in no time. This recipe makes a generous amount. Keep in the freezer and snack on it as you wish. You could use it in ice cream sandwiches, or create a simple dessert garnished with leftover cacao soil.*

ASSEMBLY: Brush ginger syrup onto the ginger cake rounds. Arrange some cacao soil and 2–3 ginger cake rounds on the plate. Add some colour with a slice of dehydrated orange (fresh is OK too) and then arrange 3 ganache logs on top of the orange and cake. When ready to serve, add a quenelle of orange ice cream, some chunks of fresh orange and fresh herbs.

ROYAL RAW GATEAUX

ROYAL RAW GATEAUX

This fancy and decadent raw chocolate gateaux has the silky smooth texture of the traditional French dessert. The shiny glaze gives it a luxurious finish, while the passionfruit centre adds a tangy element of surprise. There are quite a few components in this cake, but we promise it's worth the effort!

Makes 2 gateaux

Time: 1–1½ hours preparation, plus setting and dehydrating time

Equipment: food processor, two 10 cm (4 in) cake rings, dehydrator and mesh tray, two 2 cm (¾ in) metal rings, two 7.5 cm (3 in) metal rings, bain-marie, piping bag, high-speed blender

1 quantity chocolate syrup (see page 183)

1 quantity chocolate glaze (see page 183)

CHOCOLATE 'SPONGE'

1 flax egg (1 tablespoon flax (linseed) meal + 3 tablespoons
    filtered water)

90 g (3 oz) cashew meal

1 tablespoon cacao powder

2 tablespoons coconut sugar

4 tablespoons desiccated coconut

pinch of Himalayan pink salt

To make the flax egg, combine the flax (linseed) meal and water in a small bowl. Refrigerate for about 15 minutes until a soft gel forms.

Blitz all ingredients except the flax egg in a food processor until the mixture is super fine.

Transfer the mixture to a bowl and fold the flax egg into the dry ingredients until completely combined.

Take half the mixture and push it into one of the cake rings (this will be the cake base).

Push the other half of the mixture into the second cake ring. Dehydrate both cakes on a mesh dehydrator tray at 40°C (104°F) for 24–48 hours. The cake will have a nice crust, but it will still be quite moist on the inside.

CHOCOLATE GANACHE

1 quantity chocolate ganache (see page 183)

Prepare the ganache according to the instructions on page 183. Before setting in the fridge, pour the mixture into the bottom of two 7.5 cm (3 in) metal rings.

CHOC CRUNCH

45 g (1½ oz) bar of Pana Chocolate Raw Cacao

1 tablespoon coconut oil

1 tablespoon cacao nibs

Melt the chocolate and coconut oil together over a bain-marie. Remove from heat and stir in the cacao nibs. Pour the mixture into the metal rings that contain the chocolate ganache. Set in the fridge for 15 minutes.

PASSIONFRUIT CURD

1½ tablespoons coconut butter

2 teaspoons coconut water

1 teaspoon coconut cream

1 tablespoon passionfruit juice

2 tablespoons rice malt syrup

Blend all the ingredients together in a food processor or high-speed blender until smooth. Transfer to a bowl and refrigerate for 15 minutes to set slightly.

CHOCOLATE MOUSSE

2 × 45 g (1½ oz) bars of Pana Chocolate Raw Cacao

160 ml (5½ fl oz) coconut oil

400 ml (13½ fl oz/1⅔ cups) coconut cream

90 g (3 oz) cashews, soaked

80 ml (2½ fl oz/⅓ cup) coconut nectar

2 pinches of Himalayan pink salt

Melt the chocolate and coconut oil together over a bain-marie. Blend all the other ingredients together until the mixture is very smooth. Add the melted chocolate and oil mixture and blend until well incorporated, then set aside for assembly.

ASSEMBLY: Cut a 2.5 cm (1 in) hole in the middle of each disc of chocolate ganache and choc crunch. Pipe in the passionfruit curd to fill, then freeze for about 30 minutes. Once firm, remove the chocolate and passionfruit round from the ring and place in the middle of each sponge. Pour the chocolate mousse into and around the cake ring, to completely cover the ganache centre. Set in the freezer for approximately 1 hour, until the mousse is firm. Remove the metal ring, then place the gateaux on a wire rack and pour the chocolate glaze over the entire cake. Tap the wire rack gently on a bench to remove any excess glaze. Set the cake in the fridge, then garnish as desired before serving.

What goes round
comes round.

CHOCOLATE QUEEN OF TARTS

CHOCOLATE QUEEN OF TARTS

You can't go wrong with a classic chocolate tart, and our version hits all the right notes. This recipe makes rich, individual tarts, perfect for a glamorous afternoon tea or an impressive evening dessert. For an extra hit of flavour, incorporate your favourite Pana Chocolate bar to make the soft mousse centre even more delicious.

Makes: 5

Time: 50 minutes preparation, plus 1 hour setting time

Equipment: food processor, five 11–12 cm (4¼–4¾ in) round tart tins, bain-marie

Pana Chocolate bar shavings, to garnish

BASIC TART SHELL

    120 g (4½ oz/1⅓ cups) desiccated coconut

    125 g (4½ oz) nut flour

    50–75 ml (1¾–2½ fl oz) coconut nectar

    2 pinches of Himalayan pink salt

    coconut oil, for greasing

Blend all the ingredients except the coconut oil until the mixture comes together.

Grease the tart tins with the coconut oil, and place baking paper on the base. Press an even amount of the mixture into each tin.

Press the mixture firmly to compact it, only allowing the shell to come about 1 cm (½ in) up the sides of the tin. While you are compacting the mixture, you will notice the oils releasing – this is a great thing!

Freeze to firm up a little, then pop the shells out.

Keep the tart shells refrigerated until needed.

CHOC-MINT FILLING

45 g (1½ oz) bar of Pana Chocolate Mint

3 teaspoons coconut oil

50 g (1¾ oz) coconut butter, melted

120 ml (4 fl oz/½ cup) coconut cream

1 tablespoon coconut nectar

pinch of Himalayan pink salt

Melt the chocolate and coconut oil over a bain-marie.

Pour the melted chocolate and oil into a bowl along with all other ingredients and fold gently to combine.

Pour equal amounts of the filling into each tart shell, then return the tarts to the fridge to set for 30 minutes.

Garnish with chocolate shavings.

FREESTYLE PEAR TART

FREESTYLE PEAR TART

This moreish, free-form tart combines the sweetness of fruit and the savoury crunch of nuts. With fresh pear, our delicious vegan nut cheese and a hint of rosemary, it's a star for lunch or dinner parties. Try changing it up by using some cherry tomatoes, nut cheese and basil for a more savoury option, or swap in some fresh figs and blackberries for a twist on salty-sweet.

Makes: 7

Time: 25 minutes preparation, plus 30 minutes marinating and 8–12 hours dehydrating time

Equipment: high-speed blender, juicer/squeezer, nut milk bag

2–3 rosemary sprigs, leaves picked

edible flowers, to garnish

TART SHELL

1 quantity banana tart shell mixture (see page 182)

Prepare the tart shell mixture according to the instructions on page 182.
Divide the dough into seven equal portions.
Roll each portion out into a flat circle between two pieces of baking paper, then refrigerate until needed.

STICKY CARAMEL

50 g (1¾ oz) tahini

4 medjool dates, pitted

2 tablespoons filtered water

2 teaspoons lemon juice

1 tablespoon coconut nectar

Blend all the ingredients together until smooth. Add a little more water if the mixture becomes hard to blend. Set aside.

PEAR AND ROSEMARY FILLING

1 large pear (or 2 small pears), cut into 8 pieces lengthways

110 g (4 oz/⅓ cup) maple syrup

a few sprigs of rosemary, pounded

juice of 1 lemon

Combine the pear pieces, maple syrup, rosemary and lemon juice in a bowl and allow to marinate for about 30 minutes. Make three thin slices into each piece of pear and fan out.

Note: You will be left with an extra piece of pear, which you can divide between your tarts or use as a garnish.

MACADAMIA NUT CHEESE

125 g (4½ oz) macadamia nuts

140 ml (4½ fl oz) filtered water

1 tablespoon rice malt syrup

1½ teaspoons nutritional yeast

2 pinches of Himalayan pink salt

juice of ½ lemon

Blitz the macadamia nuts, water and rice malt syrup in a high-speed blender until smooth.

Place the mixture into a nut milk bag or muslin (cheesecloth) and squeeze the liquid out.

Place the resulting mixture (the 'cheese pulp') into a bowl and add the nutritional yeast, salt and lemon juice. Combine.

Keep the cheese in the fridge until needed.

ASSEMBLY: Spread approximately 1 tablespoon of caramel onto each rolled-out tart shell, leaving a 1 cm (½ in) border clear. Place a pear fan in the centre of each tart, then fold the tart edge in around the pear, forming a crust. Scatter small clumps of nut cheese onto and around the pear, leaving the outer crust bare. Garnish each tart with a some rosemary leaves, then place in a dehydrator at 40°C (104°F) overnight (8–10 hours). Garnish with edible flowers.

FRUITY FRANGIPANE TART

FRUITY FRANGIPANE TART

Our delicious modern take on a traditional frangipane tart combines sweet stone fruits – we love plum, but you can use any stone fruit – and thyme for garnish. Experiment with fruit and herb combinations that make your tastebuds sing.

Makes: 5

Time: 25 minutes preparation, plus 8–12 hours dehydrating time

Equipment: food processor high-speed blender, five 11–12 cm (4¼–4¾ in) tart tins, dehydrator and mesh tray

fresh fruit, sliced, to serve

baby herbs, to garnish

FLAX MEAL TART SHELL

150 g (5½ oz/1⅔ cups) desiccated coconut

50 g (1¾ oz) flax (linseed) meal

4 tablespoons coconut sugar

2 pinches of Himalayan pink salt

8 medjool dates, pitted and roughly chopped

coconut oil, for greasing

Blend the coconut, flax (linseed) meal, sugar and salt in a food processor until fine.

Add the dates to the dry ingredients one at a time, blitzing after each addition until the mixture comes together.

Grease the tart tins with coconut oil, and place baking paper on the base. Distribute the mixture evenly into the tart tins.

Press the mixture down firmly to compact it (you will notice the oils releasing through the mixture – this is a great thing!).

Place the tart shells in the freezer for 15 minutes to firm up a little, then turn them out and place them on a mesh dehydrator tray.

Dehydrate at 40°C (104°F) for 8–12 hours, or until the tart shells have firmed up.

FRANGIPANE MIX

150 g (5½ oz/1 cup) cashews, soaked

75 g (2¾ oz/⅓ cup) coconut sugar

75 ml (2½ fl oz) coconut water

pinch of Himalayan pink salt

pinch of ground cinnamon

2 vanilla beans, split lengthways and seeds scraped

105 g (3½ oz) very fine desiccated coconut

Blend all the ingredients except desiccated coconut in a
high-speed blender until very smooth.

Pour the mixture into a bowl and fold the desiccated
coconut through.

Pour equal portions of the frangipane mix into the tart shells,
then dehydrate overnight.

Top the tart with fresh fruit and pretty baby herbs.

LEMON AND BLUEBERRY TART

A recipe close to our hearts, we featured this tart in our first raw dessert masterclass, held as part of the Melbourne Food and Wine Festival in 2016. The shell is deliciously crunchy, and the lemon filling is rich and creamy. We've topped it with blueberries (we think the flavour combination is pretty hard to beat), but you could use any seasonal fruit.

Makes: 3 small tarts (or you could make one large rectangular tart instead)
Time: 20 minutes preparation, plus 8–12 hours dehydrating time
Equipment: high-speed blender, palette knife, microplane, three 11–12 cm (4¼– 4¾ in) tart tins, dehydrator and mesh tray

TART SHELL

1 quantity banana tart shell mixture (see page 182)
coconut oil, for greasing

Prepare the tart shell mixture according to the instructions on page 182.
Divide the mixture into three equal portions (skip this step if you're making one large tart).
Grease the tart tins with coconut oil, and place baking paper on the base.
Press the mixture firmly into the tart tins, then carefully de-mould and place on a mesh dehydrator tray.
Dehydrate overnight, then store at room temperature in an airtight container until needed.

LEMON CURD

80 g (2¾ oz) coconut butter
3 tablespoons lemon juice
zest of 4 lemons
pinch of Himalayan pink salt
80 ml (2½ fl oz/⅓ cup) rice malt syrup
2 tablespoons coconut oil
blueberries, to serve

Blend all the ingredients except the blueberries in a high-speed blender until very smooth.
Taste the mixture, and add more salt or rice malt syrup if needed.

ASSEMBLY: Pour equal portions of filling into each tart shell.
Arrange the blueberries (or another fruit of your choice) on top of the tarts in a small mound. Set the tarts in the fridge.

MANGO AND MACADAMIA TART

MANGO AND MACADAMIA TART

Satisfy your tropical desires with this super crunchy tart filled with creamy mango filling and topped with candied macadamia. Or opt for a totally nut-free tart with a coconut topper. Both are equally delicious, and remind us why island life would be magical.

Makes: 3

Time: 25 minutes preparation, plus 2 hours soaking, 2 hours setting and 8–12 hours dehydrating time

Equipment: three 11–12 cm (4¼–4¾ in) tart tins, food processor or high-speed blender

BUCKWHEAT TART SHELL

coconut oil, for greasing

160 g (5½ oz/1¾ cups) desiccated coconut

60 g (2 oz) activated buckwheat

60 g (2 oz) cacao butter, melted

140 ml (4½ fl oz) rice malt syrup

3 tablespoons coconut sugar

4 teaspoons baobab

Grease the tart tins with coconut oil, and place baking paper on the base.

Place all ingredients in a bowl and massage the wet ingredients into the dry ingredients until well combined.

Distribute the mixture among the tart tins, then press it in firmly and evenly.

Refrigerate for 15 minutes so the shells can firm up a little before being removed from the tins.

Keep the tart shells in the fridge until required.

MANGO CURD FILLING

100 g (3½ oz) coconut butter

80 ml (2½ fl oz/⅓ cup) coconut water

60 ml (2 fl oz/¼ cup) coconut oil

110 g (4 oz) fresh mango

2 teaspoons coconut nectar

70 ml (2¼ fl oz) rice malt syrup

juice of ½ lime

Blend all the ingredients in a high-speed blender until smooth. Divide the mixture into the prepared tart shells and keep refrigerated until serving.

MACADAMIA NUT TOPPER

25 macadamia nuts, halved

1 tablespoon maple syrup

pinch of Himalayan pink salt

3 pinches of black sesame seeds

Soak the macadamia nuts in the maple syrup and salt for 1 hour. Strain the nuts, then arrange them over three circles of baking paper the same size as the tarts. Sprinkle with the black sesame seeds.

Dehydrate at 40°C (104°F) overnight, then store in an airtight container at room temperature until needed.

COCONUT TOPPER (NUT-FREE OPTION)

40 g (1½ oz) coconut chips

3 tablespoons desiccated coconut

30 g (1 oz) maple syrup

25 g (1 oz) coconut butter, melted

Combine all the ingredients in a bowl and massage the maple syrup and coconut butter into the dry ingredients.

Arrange the mixture over three circles of baking paper the same size as the tarts.

Dehydrate at 40°C (104°F) overnight, then store in an airtight container at room temperature until needed.

ASSEMBLY: Place the coconut or macadamia nut topper (or both!) over the tarts, then serve.

STRAWBERRY BASIL TART

STRAWBERRY BASIL TART

Fresh, fruity and with show-stopping good looks, our strawberry basil tart is the perfect combination of sweet and savoury. Dehydrated cherry tomatoes add a burst of sweetness with a savoury edge, while seasonal, juicy strawberries provide colour, sweetness and plenty of zing. Topped with fragrant fresh basil, this tart is perfect for long summer nights.

Makes: 1 tart, approximately 12 × 28 cm (5 × 11 in)

Time: 25 minutes preparation, plus soaking time

Equipment: high-speed blender, bain-marie, food processor, 12 × 28 cm (4¾ × 11 in) tin, piping bag

1 quantity strawberry syrup (see page 185)

fresh strawberries, hulled and sliced, to serve

baby basil leaves, to garnish

dehydrated cherry tomatoes, to garnish

Note: The strawberry syrup recipe on page 185 makes more than enough for this recipe. Use the remainder in smoothies, chocolate fillings, on top of ice cream or however you please. Keeps well in the fridge in an airtight container or in the freezer.

NUT-FREE TART SHELL

140 g (5 oz/1½ cups) desiccated coconut

7 medjool dates, pitted

50 g (1¾ oz) flax (linseed) meal

pinch of Himalayan pink salt

Line the tin with baking paper.

Blitz all the ingredients in a food processor until the mixture comes together.

Press the mixture evenly into the tin to compact it (you will notice the oils releasing through the mixture – this is a great thing!).

Refrigerate the shell for 15 minutes so it can firm up a little before being removed from the tin.

BASIL CHEESECAKE FILLING

115 g (4 oz/¾ cup) cashews, soaked

45 ml (1½ fl oz) cashew milk

75 ml (2½ fl oz) rice malt syrup

juice of 1 lemon

65 ml (2¼ fl oz) coconut oil

8 large fresh basil leaves

Blitz all the ingredients except the coconut oil and basil leaves
in a high-speed blender until smooth.

Warm the coconut oil over a bain-marie.

Add the coconut oil to the nut mix, along with the basil leaves,
and blend until super smooth.

Pour the filling into the tart shell and set in the fridge for 1 hour.

ASSEMBLY: Arrange cut fresh strawberries on top of the tart,
then sprinkle some baby basil leaves over the top, as well as
some dehydrated cherry tomatoes. Pipe small amounts of
the strawberry syrup between some of the strawberries and
then serve.

When one dessert won't do, have petit four.

BLOOM BARS

Who doesn't love the combination of fruit and nut? A little bit chewy, a little bit crunchy, and with a delicious sweet hit, especially when it's covered in Pana Chocolate! This recipe allows you to create two different bars, depending on how you mould the mix. For a free-form look, just dip the bars in chocolate. If you'd prefer a more polished finish, you can line a chocolate mould and use the mix as a filling.

Makes: 4 bars, depending on size of moulds
Time: 10 minutes preparation, plus setting time
Equipment: four 12 × 3 cm (4¾ × 1¼ in) moulds, bain-marie

15 g (½ oz) sour cherries, chopped

13 almonds, roughly chopped

3 tablespoons pepitas (pumpkin seeds)

2 dried apricots, finely diced

45 g (1½ oz) bar of Pana Chocolate Raw Cacao, broken into pieces

Combine all the ingredients except the chocolate in a small bowl and mix them together with your fingers.

Press the mixture evenly into the moulds (the fruit should help the nuts and seeds to stick together).

Freeze the mixture for 30 minutes to make it easier to pop out of the mould.

Melt the chocolate slowly over a bain-marie.

Remove the bar mixture from the moulds and, using a fork, dip the bars into the melted chocolate.

Tap the fork against the side of the bowl to remove any excess chocolate.

Place the bar on a tray lined with baking paper and refrigerate until the chocolate has set.

Note: For a different method of presentation, line the moulds with half the melted chocolate and set in the fridge. Once set, add your seeded nut mix, then pour the remaining chocolate on top and return to the fridge. When the chocolate has set, knock out the bar.

CANNOLI

A raw, vegan take on the Italian patisserie classic, cannolis make a lovely treat for afternoon tea.
Our version teams a crispy buckwheat biscuit dipped in Pana Chocolate and nuts, with a smooth,
creamy centre. Bellissimo!

Makes: 20–30

Time: 6 hours soaking time, plus 5–10 minutes preparation,
1½ hours drying and 12–24 hours dehydrating time

Equipment: blender, dehydrator, non-stick sheet, palette knife,
metal tube or cylinder (1.5–2 cm (½–¾ in) in diametre) to shape
cannoli, bain-marie

85 g (3 oz) raw buckwheat

60 ml (2 fl oz/¼ cup) filtered water, plus extra for soaking

1 banana

2 medjool dates, pitted

45 g (1½ oz) bar of Pana Chocolate of your choice

activated nuts of your choice, finely chopped

filling of your choice

Soak the buckwheat in filtered water for at least 6 hours.
Strain and rinse thoroughly, then blend with the banana, dates
and 60 ml (2 fl oz/¼ cup) of water until smooth.

Weigh 10 g (¼ oz) of the mixture and place onto a non-stick
sheet.

Using a palette knife, form the mixture into a circle
approximately 6 cm (2½ in) in diameter.

Dehydrate for 1½ hours. When dehydrated correctly, the circles
should be flexible and easy to shape. If not, leave to dry a
little longer in the dehydrator.

Shape the cannoli over a cylindrical object, such as a rolling pin,
and stick the ends together with a little of the remaining mix.
Allow to dry overnight until crispy.

Slowly melt the chocolate over a bain-marie, then dip the ends
of the cannoli tube in the melted chocolate.

Dip the chocolate-covered ends into the chopped activated
nuts and allow to set.

Pipe filling (we love to use our chocolate mousse recipe from
the Royal Raw Gateaux, page 104) into cannoli tubes just
before serving.

Note: Raw buckwheat will swell once soaked.

CHOC-ORANGE FUDGE

This soft fudge is so versatile. Perfect as an after-dinner treat, it can also be used as a layer in a raw dessert or even as an individual chocolate filling. You can make a huge range of flavours by changing the nuts and chocolate bar flavours used, but this choc-orange version is one of our favourites.

Makes: 18 pieces

Time: 20 minutes preparation, plus 2 hours setting time

Equipment: food processor, bain-marie, 14 × 14 cm (5½ × 5½ in) brownie or cake tin, ruler

150 g (5½ oz/1 cup) raw almonds (or nut of your choice)

45 g (1½ oz) bar of Pana Chocolate of your choice, broken into pieces (note: the Raw Cacao and essential-oil flavoured bars will work best)

1 tablespoon coconut oil

2 tablespoons coconut nectar

Blend the raw almonds in a food processor on high speed until the nut butter starts to release its oils.

Scrape down the sides occasionally to ensure even blending. Transfer the nut butter to a bowl and then set aside.

Melt the chocolate bar, coconut oil and coconut nectar together over a bain-marie.

Pour the melted chocolate mix onto the nut butter and use a spatula to fold the mixture together, ensuring the ingredients are well combined.

Pour the mixture into the brownie tray or cake tin and refrigerate for 30 minutes or until set.

Using a ruler, portion the fudge into 2 × 4 cm (¾ × 1½ in) pieces.

Wrap the fudge in baking paper and keep refrigerated until serving.

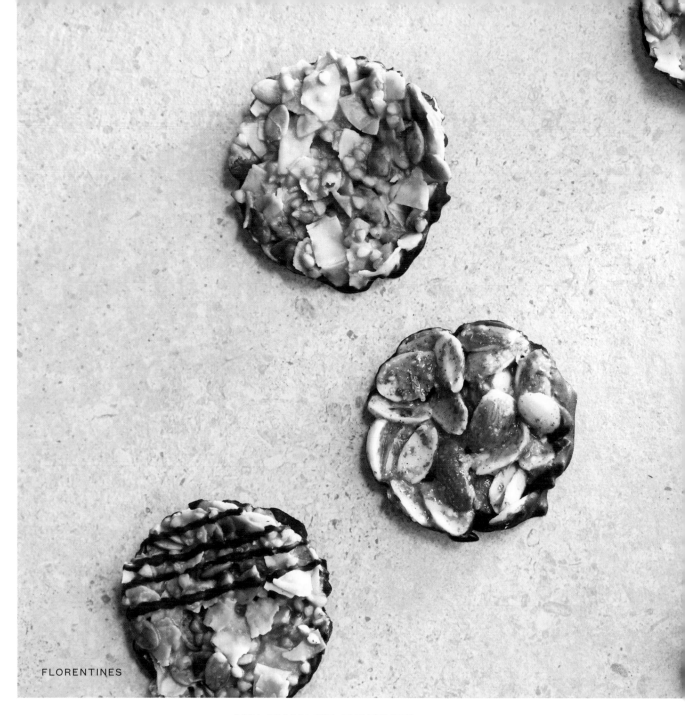

FLORENTINES

FLORENTINES

An indulgent snack, our play on the classic florentine is gooey, chewy, sweet, salty and delightful. It's simple to make and perfect as an afternoon snack. For an extra treat, dip one side of the biscuit in your favourite melted Pana Chocolate bar.

Makes: 8

Time: 25 minutes preparation, plus 8 hours dehydrating time

Equipment: food processer, 8 small metal cookie rings, dehydrator and mesh tray, bain-marie

3 × 45 g (1½ oz) bars of Pana Chocolate Raw Cacao

ALMOND CARAMEL FLORENTINE

75 g (2¾ oz/½ cup) raw almonds

2 pinches of Himalayan pink salt

85 g (3 oz/¼ cup) maple syrup

140 g (5 oz) activated almond halves

Blend the raw almonds and salt in a food processor, scraping the sides down regularly, until the nuts start to release their oils and an almond butter is formed.

Add the maple syrup to the nut butter and blend until fully incorporated to form an almond caramel.

Add 4 tablespoons of the almond caramel to a bowl with the activated almond halves, and massage the caramel into the nuts to coat.

Place the metal cookie rings on a mesh dehydrator tray, then divide the almond halves among the rings and arrange them flat side-up in each ring. Slightly overlap the almond halves so the biscuit will hold its shape.

Dehydrate at 40°C (104°F) overnight (for at least 8 hours).

SUPERSEED FLORENTINE

60 g (2 oz) tahini

335 g (12 oz/1 cup) maple syrup

4 tablespoons pepitas (pumpkin seeds)

4 tablespoons coconut chips

2 tablespoons activated buckwheat

Combine the tahini and maple syrup until fully incorporated to make a tahini caramel.

Combine all the remaining ingredients in a bowl, then add 4 tablespoons of the tahini caramel and massage it into the dry ingredients.

Press the mixture into the eight metal cookie rings sitting on a dehydrator tray.

Dehydrate overnight (for at least 8 hours).

Note: You can use the remaining caramel as a sweet treat on toast.

ASSEMBLY: Slowly melt the chocolate over a bain-marie. Once melted, dip the bottom side of each florentine into the chocolate. Place face down on a tray and allow to set. Once set, flip each florentine over and drizzle chocolate over the top. Allow to set.

ICE CREAM POPS

Is there anything more tantalising on a hot summer's day than the cool, sticky hit of ice cream? We love it too, so we've created our own mini ice cream pops. You can make these using our coconut ice cream recipe (page 184), our orange ice cream recipe (page 101), or a store-bought alternative. Make them special with a crisp Pana Chocolate coating, and stud them with nuts, berries or coconut to give them extra wow factor.

Makes: 20–25

Time: 10 minutes preparation, plus 2 hours setting time

Equipment: tray, toothpicks, bain-marie

coconut ice cream (see page 184, or use a
    store-bought dairy-free version), or another flavour of
    your choice
45 g (1½ oz) bar of Pana Chocolate Raw Cacao, broken
    into pieces (or use an essential-oil chocolate for a hit of
    flavour – try Orange, Mint, Rose or Cinnamon)
garnish of your choice – nuts, berries and/or coconut

Before you start, place your tray in the freezer to chill.

Scoop small portions of ice cream with a tablespoon, or use a mini ice cream scoop to help!

Working quickly, roll the ice cream portions into balls using your hands.

Place the ice cream balls on the cold tray and insert a toothpick inside each ball. Freeze until very hard.

Melt the chocolate slowly over a bain-marie, then dip each ice cream ball into the melted chocolate.

Roll the balls in your chosen garnish, then refreeze.

MINI LAMOS

MINI LAMOS

Our mini lamos use components of the traditional lamington – think a raspberry mousse,
a layer of chocolate and a dousing of desiccated coconut. For this perfect bite-size treat, we use
coconut and cacao to create a delicious mousse texture. You can top with fresh raspberries for
extra zing.

Makes: approximately 15

Time: 25 minutes preparation, plus 4 hours setting and
20 minutes assembly time

Equipment: food processor or high-speed blender, bain-marie,
13 × 9 cm (5 × 3½ in) brownie or cake tin, chopstick (or similar)

1 quantity raspberry jam (see page 184)

dessicated coconut

3 × 45 g (1½ oz) bars of Pana Chocolate Raw Cacao, optional
(if you would prefer not to dip in chocolate, the coconut will
stick to the ganache)

1 teaspoon coconut oil

RASPBERRY CHOCOLATE GANACHE

170 g (6 oz) fresh or frozen raspberries

60 ml (2 fl oz) coconut oil

150 g (5¼/1 cup) cashews, soaked

90 ml (3 fl oz) coconut nectar

4 tablespoons cacao powder

1 vanilla bean, split lengthways and seeds scraped

pinch of Himalayan pink salt

Blend the raspberries in a high-speed blender until smooth,
then strain to remove the seeds and set aside.
Melt the coconut oil over a bain-marie.
Blend the cashews in a food processor, scraping down the
sides regularly, until the oils are released and the mixture has
achieved a butter-like consistency.

Return the raspberry purée to the blender along with the cashew butter and all remaining ingredients except the coconut oil.

Blend the mixture until smooth, then add the melted coconut oil and blend the mixture again.

Pour the ganache into the cake or brownie tin. For perfectly square bites, the mixture should reach approximately 2.5 cm (1 in) up the side.

Set in the freezer, then turn the ganache out onto a cutting board and portion it into 2.5 × 2.5 cm (1 × 1 in) pieces.

Use a chopstick to make a hole in the centre of each piece, being careful not to poke through the bottom. Twist the chopstick gently to make the hole a little larger.

Place the ganache onto a tray and into the fridge until you are ready to assemble your mini lamos.

ASSEMBLY: Pipe raspberry jam into the hole in each ganache square until full. Fill a bowl with desiccated coconut. Melt the chocolate over a bain-marie. Add a little coconut oil (approximately 1 teaspoon) to the chocolate to give it an extra smooth consistency. Using a fork, dip each ganache square into the chocolate. Tap the fork against the bowl to remove the excess chocolate, then drop the ganache square into the coconut. Shake the bowl to cover the square completely in coconut. Repeat for all squares, then refrigerate until needed.

MINI MERINGUE PIES

MINI MERINGUE PIES

We love these bite-size treats with crunchy biscuit casing, zesty lemon curd and a soft coconut cream meringue top. The lemon curd filling is versatile – we use it for raw dessert cake layers and even individual chocolate fillings. Experiment with alternate citrus flavours if you like – limes or oranges also work well.

Makes: 11 mini tarts

Time: 25 minutes preparation, plus 30 minutes setting and 12–24 hours dehydrating time

Equipment: eleven 4–5 cm (1½–2 in) tart tins, dehydrator with mesh tray, bain-marie high-speed blender, paper bag

CHOCOLATE TART SHELL

50 g (1¾ oz) wet nut milk pulp

1 tablespoon desiccated coconut

1 tablespoon coconut sugar

1 tablespoon cacao powder

Using your hands, massage all ingredients together in a small bowl.

Divide the mixture into eleven equal portions and press into the tart tins, then freeze for 15 minutes. Once the shells are frozen, pop them out of the moulds and place on a mesh dehydrator tray. Dehydrate at 40°C (104°F) for 12–24 hours.

Allow to cool.

LEMON CURD

    60 ml (2 fl oz) coconut oil

    40 g (1½ oz/¼ cup) cashews, soaked

    80 ml (2½ fl oz/⅓ cup) rice malt syrup

    juice and zest of 1 large lemon

    pinch of Himalayan pink salt

    pinch of ground turmeric

Melt the coconut oil over a bain-marie.

Blend all the ingredients except the coconut oil in a high-speed blender until smooth.

Add the coconut oil and blend until very smooth.

Pour equal portions of the mixture into each tart shell and set in the fridge for 30 minutes.

COCONUT CREAM MERINGUE

    400 ml (13½ fl oz) coconut cream

    1 tablespoon coconut oil

    1 teaspoon rice malt syrup

    coconut sugar, for sprinkling

Refrigerate the coconut cream overnight.

Melt the coconut oil over a bain-marie.

Scoop the solid cream off the top of the coconut cream and place the solid cream in a chilled bowl (discard the leftover water). Add the rice malt syrup and whisk to combine.

While whisking, pour the coconut oil into the cream, continuing to whisk so the oil sets evenly.

Transfer the mixture to a piping bag and pipe a little meringue onto the top of each tart.

Sprinkle a tiny bit of coconut sugar over each meringue.

Refrigerate until needed, or serve immediately.

RAWRONS

These soft sandwich cookies are the perfect raw version of the modern-day macaron. They can be made with any filling – we love nut butter, fruit chia jams, our ganache, and homemade caramel. For more options, explore our chocolate fillings section on pages 30–47.

Makes: 20–25

Time: 30 minutes preparation, plus soaking time and 12–24 hours dehydrating time

Equipment: blender, food processor or spice grinder, piping bag, dehydrator with mesh tray, bain-marie

75 g (2¾ oz/½ cup) cashews, soaked

60 ml (2 fl oz/¼ cup) filtered water

3 tablespoons coconut sugar

2 teaspoons cacao powder

25 g (1 oz) nut flour (see note)

25 g (1 oz) desiccated coconut

Blend the cashews, water, coconut sugar and cacao powder in a high-speed blender until smooth, then transfer the mixture to a bowl.

Blitz the desiccated coconut and nut flour together in a food processor until very fine.

Fold the coconut and nut flour mix into the cashew mix.

Transfer the mixture to a piping bag and pipe small rounds approximately 2.5 cm (1 in) in diameter onto a mesh dehydrator tray or baking paper-lined tray.

Dehydrate the biscuits at 40°C (104°F) for 12–24 hours, then remove and allow to cool.

Pipe your desired filling onto half of the biscuits and sandwich them together with a top biscuit.

Serve immediately.

Note: These biscuits will keep well without filling, in an airtight container in a cool, dry place.

Made for kids. But who are we kidding.

CACAO CRACKLES

Remember the chocolate crackles from your sixth birthday party? These crunchy bite-size crackles are the perfect, healthy alternative for kids' parties or school lunch boxes. Best of all, they're completely nut free. Dip them in a melted chocolate bar of your choice – if you're anything like us, you'll have trouble sharing them with the kids.

Makes: 6

Time: 15 minutes preparation, plus 8–12 hours dehydrating time

Equipment: bain-marie, dehydrator, non-stick sheet

3 teaspoons chocolate
    syrup (see page 183)
35 g (1¼ oz) puffed millet
45 g (1½ oz) bar of Pana
    Chocolate of your
    choice,
    broken into pieces

Combine the chocolate syrup and puffed millet in a bowl, and stir to ensure the millet is well coated.

Roll the mixture into tablespoon-sized balls.

Place the balls on a dehydrator tray and dehydrate at 40°C (104°F) for 8–12 hours.

Line a tray with baking paper.

Melt the chocolate bar over a bain-marie.

Drop the dehydrated crackles into the melted chocolate, coating thoroughly.

Use a fork to retrieve the crackles. Tap the fork on the side of the bowl to remove any excess chocolate.

Set the crackles on the lined tray in the refrigerator for about 15 minutes, or until the chocolate is set.

Serve in little paper cases, if desired.

NOT HONEY JOYS

A bite-size vegan take on the classic, these sweet, crispy coconut morsels are a lovely addition to children's birthday parties and make great lunch box treats for kids and adults alike. And they're entirely nut free, making them safe for kids with nut allergies, too. Drizzle with melted chocolate for an added flavour hit.

Makes: approximately 10

Time: 10–20 minutes preparation, plus 8–12 hours dehydrating time

Equipment: food processor or high-speed blender, dehydrator, non-stick sheet

1 tablespoon goji berries

filtered water, for soaking

3 tablespoons coconut nectar

10 g (¼ oz) coconut butter, melted

40 g (1½ oz) coconut chips

3 tablespoons desiccated coconut

Soak the goji berries in filtered water (enough just to cover). Once the berries are moist and plump, combine the berries, 2 teaspoons of the soaking juice and the coconut nectar and blend until smooth.

Pour the blended berries into a bowl. Add the coconut butter, chips and desiccated coconut and massage together.

Divide the mixture into ten equal portions and press each together into compact balls.

Place the portions on a non-stick sheet and dehydrate at 40°C (104°F) overnight.

Place in little paper cases if desired.

NICE CRISPIES

The old-fashioned rice crispy treats are always a winner at kids' parties. We've added a raw twist and used activated buckwheat to give our crispies a hearty crunch, using chewy, sweet caramel to bind the mixture together. Another great recipe for children with allergies, our nice crispies are nut-free and delicious.

Makes: 16

Time: 10 minutes preparation, plus 1 hour setting time

Equipment: bain-marie, 20 × 20 cm (8 × 8 in) brownie or cake tin, palette knife

2 tablespoons coconut butter

2 tablespoons coconut oil

4 tablespoons tahini

130 ml (4½ fl oz) coconut nectar

60 g (2 oz) puffed millet

200 g (7 oz) activated buckwheat

Melt the coconut butter and coconut oil together over a bain-marie.

Take the mixture off the heat and stir in the tahini and coconut nectar.

Pour the mixture into a bowl along with the puffed millet and activated buckwheat and stir to combine.

Pour the mixture into the brownie or cake tin and smooth out with a palette knife.

Refrigerate until firm, then portion into 4 × 4 cm (1½ × 1½ in) squares.

SMILING COOKIES

Get happy with these cute, smiley vanilla coconut cookie sandwiches. Nut-free, simple to make and easy to fill with caramel or jam, these are a cheery treat for kids and big kids alike. If you want to make them extra special, try dipping them in melted chocolate.

Makes: 20–25

Time: 30 minutes preparation, plus 8–12 hours dehydration time

Equipment: food processor, dehydrator and mesh tray, 5 cm (2 in) cookie cutter

125 g (4½ oz) activated buckwheat flour

155 g (5½ oz) desiccated coconut

2 tablespoons coconut nectar

1 tablespoon coconut oil

1 vanilla bean, split lengthways and seeds scraped

2 tablespoons filtered water

Blitz the dry ingredients in a food processor until fine.

Add the coconut nectar, coconut oil, vanilla seeds and water and blitz until the mixture forms a dough.

Roll out the dough between two sheets of baking paper.

Using the cookie cutter, cut the dough into an even number of circles, then refrigerate for 15 minutes to firm up a little.

Cut the eyes and mouths out of half of the circles, leaving the other half plain (these will be the backs of the cookie).

Return the circles to the refrigerator to firm up before transferring them onto a mesh dehydrator tray. Dehydrate for 12 hours.

Spread the filling of your choice (one of our favourites is the raspberry jam on page 184) onto each plain cookie, then add a face cookie on top, sandwiching the two together. Serve immediately.

Easter. Christmas. Valentine's. Tuesday. Whenever.

CARAMEL LAVA EGG

Quite frankly, there are simply not enough holidays for celebrating and appreciating the beauty of chocolate. We can only think of four, which is a disgrace. Now you can celebrate all year round with our popular caramel lava egg. These are a hot commodity among healthified chocoholics, and sell out within hours of their Easter release. They even spearheaded the beginning of our favourite new holiday, Faux Easter – like Christmas in July, just with way more chocolate!

Makes: approximately 8 medium eggs

Time: 20 minutes preparation, plus 2 hours setting time

Equipment: high-speed blender, fine sieve, 7 cm (2¾ in) chocolate egg moulds (or similar)

11 medjool dates, pitted

85 ml (2¾ fl oz) filtered water

1½ tablespoons lemon juice

2 tablespoons coconut sugar

1½ tablespoons coconut butter

1 tablespoon tahini

2 pinches of Himalayan pink salt

2–3 45 g (1½ oz) bars of Pana Chocolate Raw Cacao

Line the chocolate egg moulds (follow the instructions for making individual chocolates on pages 25–26).

To create a date paste, blend the medjool dates, filtered water and 1 tablespoon of the lemon juice in a high-speed blender until smooth. Pass through a fine sieve, if desired. Set aside.

Combine the coconut sugar and the remaining ½ tablespoon of lemon juice in a bowl. Mix until the sugar dissolves.

Fold together the coconut butter, tahini, salt and 80 g (2¾ oz) of the date paste.

Transfer the mixture into a piping bag and pipe into each lined chocolate mould.

Close the moulds with chocolate and set in the fridge for 2 hours. Once set, knock the chocolates out of the moulds.

Note: *You could also make approximately 28 small individual chocolates with the caramel filling by following the instructions on pages 25–26.*

The date paste recipe will make more than is required for your caramel lava eggs. The excess can be used as a sweetener in raw cakes, smoothies or nut milk, or you can spread it on toast or banana bread.

CHOC-CHERRY HOT CROSS BUNS

An Easter staple, hot cross buns are a spicy, delicious treat. As much as we appreciate the traditional version, we think our buns with a choc-cherry twist are even better. Serve them toasted with a sliver of nut butter for afternoon tea, or pack them for lunch – they're perfect either way.

Makes: 18

Time: 25 minutes preparation, plus 12 hours dehydrating time

Equipment: high-speed blender, dehydrator, non-stick sheet, piping bag

65 g (2¼ oz) psyllium husk

200 g (7 oz) Brazil nut pulp

1 tablespoon ground cinnamon

1 teaspoon ground nutmeg

1 teaspoon ground ginger

1 vanilla bean, split lengthways and seeds scraped

70 g (2½ oz) flax (linseed) meal

150 g (5½ oz/⅔ cup) coconut sugar

2 pinches of Himalayan pink salt

165 g (6 oz/1 cup) chopped medjool dates

1 tablespoon maple syrup, plus extra for glazing

220 ml (7½ fl oz) filtered water

80 g (2¾ oz) sour cherries

35 g (1¼ oz) dried cranberries

100 g (3½ oz) Pana Chocolate Raw Cacao, broken into chunks

for the chocolate cross:

120 g (4½ oz/¾ cup) cashews, soaked

2 tablespoons filtered water

2 tablespoons cacao powder

In a bowl, combine the psyllium, Brazil nut pulp, spices, vanilla seeds, flax (linseed) meal, coconut sugar and salt. Ensure there are no clumps in the mixture.

Pulse the dates in a high-speed blender until they form a chunky paste (approximately 4–5 seconds).

Add the maple syrup, filtered water and date mixture to the dry mix and massage together with your hands until combined.

Continuing to use your hands, fold through the sour cherries, cranberries and chocolate chunks.

Form the mixture into balls of approximately 3 tablespoons each, and place them on a non-stick sheet, leaving a few centimetres/an inch between each.

Using a pastry brush, glaze each bun with maple syrup (not too much – they shouldn't be dripping).

To make the mixture for the chocolate cross, blend the cashews, water and cacao powder until smooth.

Using a piping bag with a small nozzle, pipe the mixture into a cross onto the top of each bun.

Dehydrate the buns at 40°C (104°F) for at least 12 hours.

CHRISTMAS PUDDING

Raw sweetness, spice and all things nice, our delicious Christmas puddings take the cake, every festive season. Combine our mince tart filling with cinnamon, ginger and nutmeg to create these dreamy puddings. Serve with ice cream or top with your favourite melted Pana Chocolate for extra tastiness.

Makes: 2 puddings

Time: 35 minutes preparation, plus 8–10 hours soaking and 8–10 hours dehydrating time

Equipment: 2 pudding moulds or bowls

165 g (6 oz) Brazil nut flour (from nut milk pulp)

160 g (5½ oz) fine cashew meal

22 g (¾ oz) lacuma powder

1 tablespoon ground nutmeg

1 tablespoon ground ginger

1 tablespoon ground cinnamon

230 g (8 oz) medjool dates, pitted and chopped

100 ml (3½ fl oz) fresh orange juice with pulp

1 tablespoon coconut nectar

200 g (7 oz) Pana mince tart filling (see page 173)

45 g (1½ oz) bar of Pana Chocolate Raw Cacao, broken into pieces

dehydrated fruit, to garnish

nuts, to garnish

baby herbs, to garnish

Combine the nut flours, lacuma powder and spices in a bowl.

Blend the dates, orange juice and coconut nectar in a food processor until the mixture forms a paste.

Add the date mixture to the dry ingredients and massage together until combined.

Add the mince tart filling and massage again to combine.

Place half the mixture into each pudding mould or bowl and press it down firmly.

Refrigerate overnight, then tip the pudding out of the mould.

Melt the chocolate over a bain marie, and drizzle over the pudding. Garnish with dehydrated fruit, nuts and baby herbs of your choice.

MAGIC MINCE TARTS

Mince tarts are the perfect Christmas treat, but can often be laden with sugars and additives. This silly season, swap the nasties for a hit of raw, festive goodness using this twist on the traditional recipe. Your Christmas guests won't believe how good they are.

Makes: 30 tarts

Time: 20 minutes preparation, plus 8–11 hours dehydrating and soaking time

Equipment: food processor, star-shaped cookie cutter, small tart tins or pan, dehydrator with mesh tray

TART SHELL

1 quantity banana tart shell mixture (see page 182)

Prepare the tart shell mixture according to the instructions on page 182.

Firmly press approximately 20 g (¾ oz) of the mixture into the tart tins to shape, then carefully remove the tarts from their moulds and place on a mesh dehydrator tray.

The remaining mixture will form the tops of your tarts. Roll it between two sheets of baking paper, then use the star cookie cutter to cut out stars.

Dehydrate the shells and stars at 40°C (104°F) overnight (8–10 hours) on a mesh dehydrator tray, making sure the tart is dry. Allow extra time if it is not completely dry. Remove the tart shells when ready to use.

Note: If you are looking to keep the crunch of the star, brush the back of each star with melted chocolate and set before placing on the tart.

PANA MINCE TART FILLING

10 medjool dates, pitted and chopped

20 g (¾ oz) goji berries

50 g (1¾ oz) blueberries

3 tablespoons coconut sugar

120 ml (4 fl oz/½ cup) fresh orange juice with pulp

1 tablespoon ground cinnamon

pinch of ground ginger

pinch of ground nutmeg

pinch of Himalayan pink salt

150 g (5½ oz) prunes, chopped into small pieces

Soak the dates, goji berries, blueberries and coconut sugar in orange juice for at least 1 hour.

Blitz the soaked mixture in a food processor until gently combined, being careful not to blend it to a paste.

Add the spices, salt and prunes to the food processor and blitz for 2–3 seconds.

ASSEMBLY: Divide the mince tart filling among the tart shells. Place the stars on top of the tarts while the mince is still wet so it holds them in place.

SPICED PUMPKIN TARTS

SPICED PUMPKIN TARTS

Adding pumpkin (winter squash) to your desserts is a great way to get your daily serving of vegies. Being quite a sweet vegetable, pumpkin is a great option when making this raw tart. The addition of chocolate, spices and coconut cream makes this dessert quite decadent.

Makes: 7

Time: 20 minutes preparation

Equipment: food processor, seven 7 cm (2¾ in) small tart tins, bain-marie, palette knife

45 g (1½ oz) bar of Pana Chocolate Cinnamon, broken into 6 pieces

1 teaspoon coconut oil

1 quantity whipped coconut cream (see page 185)

TART SHELL

60 g (2 oz) Brazil nut flour

60 g (2 oz/⅔ cup) desiccated coconut

1 tablespoon cacao powder

pinch of Himalayan pink salt

2 medjool dates, pitted

Blitz the nut flour, coconut, cacao powder and salt in a high-speed blender.

Add the dates and pulse until the mixture comes together.

Be careful not to over blitz; otherwise, the mixture will become too oily.

Divide the the mixture into the tart tins and press down to create the tart shells.

Freeze shells until needed.

PUMPKIN PIE FILLING

100 g (3½ oz/⅔ cup) cashews, soaked

100 g (3½ oz) coconut butter, melted

100 g (3½ oz) raw pumpkin (winter squash), puréed

2 tablespoons coconut sugar

30 ml (1 fl oz) coconut nectar

1 tablespoon ground nutmeg

1 tablespoon ground cinnamon

1 tablespoon ground ginger

1 teaspoon ground clove

pinch of Himalayan pink salt

Drain the soaked cashews and blend in a high-speed blender along with all the other ingredients until well incorporated and very smooth.

Taste the mixture, and adjust spices if needed.

Note: This recipe makes enough to fill 10 tart shells, so you will have a little left over.

ASSEMBLY: Melt 5 of the chocolate squares with the coconut oil over a bain-marie. Brush the inside of each tart shell with the melted chocolate, then return to the fridge or freezer to set the chocolate. Pour some pumpkin filling into each tart shell and smooth with a palette knife, then set in the refrigerator. Place or drizzle 1 teaspoon of whipped coconut cream onto each tart, then grate the remaining chocolate over the top.

SWEETHEART DONUTS

Donut worry, be happy. See what we did there? These stunning raw vegan donuts are one of a kind, delightful in flavour with a shimmery glaze. Perfect to share with that special someone (or not, we don't judge).

Makes: 12

Time: 25 minutes preparation, plus 12 hours dehydrating time

Equipment: food processor, mini donut mould/tin (or similar), dehydrator, bain-marie

1 quantity chocolate glaze (see page 183)

dehydrated rose petals, to garnish

DONUT DOUGH

80 g (2¾ oz) cashew meal

60 g (2 oz/⅔ cup) desiccated coconut

45 g (1½ oz) activated buckwheat flour

45 g (1½ oz) Brazil nut flour

pinch of Himalayan pink salt

juice and zest of ½ lemon

45 ml (1½ fl oz) coconut nectar

1 drop of lemon essential oil

Blitz the cashew meal, desiccated coconut, buckwheat flour and Brazil nut flour in a food processor until fine.

Transfer the mixture to a bowl, then add salt, lemon zest and juice, coconut nectar and lemon essential oil. Massage the mixture with your hands to combine.

If you own a donut mould tin, divide the dough into heaped tablespoon-sized portions and roll each portion into a ball. Push each portion down into the tin to ensure it takes the donut shape, then tap out onto the bench. If you don't have a donut mould, roll the dough out between two sheets of baking paper until it is 2 cm (¾ in) thick, then cut out using a 4 cm (1½ in) cookie cutter. Cut a hole approximately 1 cm (½ in) in the middle of each donut.

Place the donuts on a dehydrator tray and dehydrate at 40°C (104°F) for 12 hours.

ASSEMBLY: Carefully dip each of your donuts into the glaze. Garnish with dehydrated rose petals.

Note: *If you prefer, you can also eat this donut mixture without dehydrating it – just set it in the fridge for 15 minutes.*

Go the extra page.
It's worth it.

BANANA TART SHELL

120 g (4½ oz) banana

60 g (2 oz/¼ cup) maple syrup

1 vanilla bean, split lengthways and seeds scraped

pinch of Himalayan pink salt

65 g (2¼ oz/¾ cup) desiccated coconut

65 g (2¼ oz) nut flour

40 g (1½ oz) flax (linseed) meal

Blitz the banana, maple syrup, vanilla seeds and salt together in a high-speed blender.

Pour the mixture into a bowl and fold the coconut, nut flour and flax (linseed) meal through.

Divide the dough into portions as needed and refrigerate until required.

BERRY COMPOTE

½ cup mixed berries, either fresh or frozen

peel of ½ lemon

½ vanilla bean, split lengthways and seeds scraped

1 teaspoon coconut sugar

Combine all the ingredients in a bowl and marinate at room temperature for 1 hour. This should be sufficient time for the coconut sugar to dissolve and the fruit to take on hints of citrus and vanilla. Remove the lemon peel when serving.

This compote can be stored in an airtight container in the fridge for 3–4 days.

BUTTERSCOTCH SAUCE

100 ml (3½ fl oz) Brazil nut milk (see page 184, or use store-bought)

50 g (1¾ oz) cacao butter, melted

120 g (4¼ oz) coconut sugar

4 tablespoons lacuma powder

Whisk all the ingredients together in a bowl.

Store in the fridge until needed, or use straight away.

CANDY NUT SHARD

100 g (3½ oz/⅔ cup) almonds

100 ml (3½ fl oz) coconut nectar

50 ml (1¾ fl oz) filtered water

Blitz the almonds in a food processor until finely chopped.

Place the nuts in a fine sieve and shake off excess nut meal, leaving nicely clean chopped nuts.

Combine the chopped nuts in a bowl with coconut nectar and water and stir to coat.

Cover and allow to sit for a couple of hours, then pour the mixture into a sieve and drain the liquid.

Place the nuts onto a non-stick sheet and dehydrate at 40°C (104°F) overnight.

Flip the nuts after a couple of hours to ensure they dry evenly.

Allow to cool, then break into shards

CHOCOLATE GANACHE

45 g (1½ oz) bar of Pana Chocolate Raw Cacao (or choose a flavoured chocolate if you want to flavour your ganache)

1¼ tablespoons nut milk (see page 184, or use store bought)

Melt the chocolate and nut milk together over a bain-marie. Try not to stir the mixture too much, or it will split.

Transfer the mixture to a bowl and then set in the fridge for about 15 minutes.

CHOCOLATE GLAZE

1¼ tablespoons coconut oil

2 tablespoons cacao butter

100 ml (3½ oz) chocolate syrup (see recipe at right)

Melt the coconut oil and cacao butter together over a bain-marie. Add the melted oil and butter mixture with the chocolate syrup and stir thoroughly. Make sure the syrup is at room temperature (or warm over a bain-marie) before combining, or the mixture may seize.

CHOCOLATE SHARD

45 g (1½ oz) bar of Pana Chocolate Orange, broken into pieces

1 teaspoon coconut oil

1 dried fig, cut into small squares

2 slices of dehydrated orange, cut into small wedges

Melt the chocolate and coconut oil over a bain-marie. While the mixture is melting, cover a baking tray with a sheet of baking paper. Pour the mixture onto the tray.

Scatter fig and orange over the melted chocolate and then set it in the fridge for at least 2 hours, until needed. Break into shards to serve.

CHOCOLATE SYRUP

90 g (3¼ oz/¾ cup) cacao powder

140 ml (4½ fl oz) coconut nectar

100 ml (3½ fl oz) filtered water

Place all the ingredients into a bowl and whisk together until smooth and shiny.

COCONUT CRUMBLE

100 g (3½ oz) coconut chips

50 g (1¾ oz) nut flour

50 ml (1¾ fl oz) coconut nectar

Pulse the coconut chips in a food processor to break up slightly. Pour into a bowl and add the nut flour and coconut nectar. Massage the coconut nectar into the dry ingredients until evenly coated. Allow the mixture to clump together.

Place on a mesh dehydrator tray and dehydrate at 40°C (104°F) for 24 hours. Store in an airtight container.

COCONUT ICE CREAM

80 ml (2½ fl oz) coconut cream

50 g (1¾ oz) coconut meat

150 ml (5 fl oz) coconut water

80 ml (2½ fl oz) rice malt syrup

40 ml (1¼ fl oz) coconut oil, melted over a bain-marie

Blend all the ingredients except for the coconut oil in a high-speed blender until extra smooth.

Add the melted coconut oil and blend until the oil has been well incorporated and the mixture is very smooth.

Pour the mixture into a shallow container and freeze overnight.

Scoop the frozen mixture into a food processor, then blitz to break up the ice crystals, making the ice cream smooth.

Scoop the ice cream and serve immediately.

NUT BUTTER

nuts of your choice (1 cup raw nuts will make ½ cup nut butter)

Blend the nuts in a food processor on high until the oils are released and the mixture resembles butter. Constantly scrape down the sides to ensure even blending. Results may vary depending on the nuts you use.

Season with salt or a little vanilla, if desired.

NUT MILK

2½ cups nuts of your choice, soaked (see page 27 for information on how long to soak different types of nuts)

1 litre (34 fl oz/4 cups) filtered water

Combine the soaked nuts and filtered water in a high-speed blender. Blend for 30 seconds, then strain the mixture in a nut milk bag or muslin (cheesecloth), making sure to catch the nut milk in a bowl underneath. Squeeze the bag or cloth to remove all the milk, and reserve the pulp for use in other recipes.

PEAR CHIP

1 small pear

juice of 1 lemon

Cut the pear into slices approximately 5 mm (¼ in) thick using a mandolin or a knife.

Coat the sliced pear with a little lemon juice to stop the fruit from oxidising, then place on a dehydrator tray and dehydrate at 40°C (104°F) overnight (or at least 8 hours).

RASPBERRY JAM

150 g (5½ oz) fresh or frozen raspberries

40 ml (1¼ fl oz) rice malt syrup

zest and juice of ½ lime

2 tablespoons chia seeds

45 g (1½ oz) fresh raspberries

Defrost the raspberries, if necessary.

Blend the raspberries in a high-speed blender with the rice malt syrup and lime zest and juice until smooth.

Pour the mixture into a bowl and fold the chia seeds through.

Allow to thicken in the fridge for 2 hours, then fold the fresh raspberries through.

REJUVELAC

50 g (1¾ oz/¼ cup) quinoa

filtered water (enough to cover the quinoa well)

Thoroughly rinse the quinoa, then soak in water for 6–8 hours.

Rinse the quinoa, then place in a clean bowl and cover with a damp cloth.

Allow the quinoa to sprout – this will usually take 2 days.

Rinse the sprouted quinoa thoroughly again, then place it in a clean jar and fill with 500 ml (17 fl oz/2 cups) of water. Cover the jar with a cloth and allow the quinoa to ferment for a couple of days.

When it's ready, the liquid will become slightly 'fizzy' and have a slight lemony taste.

Strain the liquid into a clean jar, seal with a lid and keep in the fridge for 5–7 days.

STRAWBERRY SYRUP

165 g (6 oz) fresh strawberries

juice of ½ lemon

3 medjool dates, pitted

pinch of Himalayan pink salt

1 vanilla bean, split lengthways and seeds scraped

Blend all the ingredients in a high-speed blender until the mixture is super smooth.

Store the syrup in the fridge until needed.

VANILLA CUSTARD

100 g (3½ oz/⅔ cup) cashews, soaked

80 ml (2½ fl oz) coconut cream

2 teaspoons rice malt syrup

pinch of Himalayan pink salt

1 vanilla bean, split lengthways and seeds scraped

Place all ingredients into a high-speed blender and blend on high until very smooth.

Place the mixture in a container until needed.

WHIPPED COCONUT CREAM

400 ml (13½ fl oz) coconut cream

sweetener of your choice, to taste

1 vanilla bean, split lengthways and seeds scraped

Refrigerate the coconut cream overnight.

Drain any remaining liquid from the cream, then pour the solidified cream into a chilled bowl, along with the sweetener and vanilla seeds.

Whisk the mixture with an electric beater until it resembles whipped cream. Be careful not to over whisk, as this will melt the cream, causing it to collapse.

Refrigerate until needed.

Index

Who is Pana?

To Pana Barbounis, food is everything. It's medicine. It's experience. It's love.

Born in Australia to Greek parents, Pana grew up in a family that was, in true European style, passionate about sharing food, stories and experiences. His upbringing instilled in him a strong sense of community and a love of wholesome, nourishing ingredients.

He began his hospitality career at age 16, as a kitchen hand. Pana was hungry to learn and, by 21, he'd launched his first business.

His enterprises continued to evolve, from cafes and catering to vineyard restaurants, but in his thirties, he felt drawn to return to his passion: making things. He began experimenting with raw chocolate recipes and, from determination, patience and love, Pana Chocolate was born.

Despite growing up in a 'lamb and feta cheese' household, Pana now embraces a wholly sustainable and vegan life. When he's not testing new recipes with the Pana Chocolate team, he's zipping around Melbourne on his Vespa, practising yoga, cooking, and spending time with family and friends.

Pana believes that connection, experience and joy are fundamental to a happy life, and that food, stories and wisdom are what unite us.

Thank you

This is a huge milestone for Pana Chocolate, and for myself. There have been so many wonderful moments on this journey, and none were more satisfying than those I shared with the people who have made it possible – you! Thank you for your continued support, for loving quality chocolate and for caring about yourself and the earth. Oh, and for continually asking us for recipes. Here they are!

None of this would have been possible without the gorgeous, inspiring and passionate team behind me: my original team, who is still with me – Maria, Kumari and Ranjani – and the ever motivated, caring, creative, hardworking and happy team of makers, wrappers, packers, and workers in operations, sales, marketing, human resources, finance, customer service, the shops and the raw kitchen. Love you all to bits (chocolate bits)!

A massive thank you goes to our incredible chef talent, including our masterful product development chef, Amber Wood, who led this project. Amber, you are a super talent who has made many dreams come true and many customers happy with your unbelievable creations over the years. Thank you for continually delivering above and beyond, and for what you have brought to Pana Chocolate.

There are a bunch of other really important people who also deserve some love for all their support: Pana Chocolate's first ever stockists; our current stockists; our amazing distributors (past and present); book project coordinators Amanda Bevan and Ashleigh Walker; my best friend, Elaine So; my sister, Maria Barbounis; and my partner, co-decision-maker and the mother of my three gorgeous kids (Olivia, Tahlia and James), Yola Barbounis.

Thank you all from the bottom of my heart.

Pana Barbounis

AMBER WOOD, PRODUCT DEVELOPMENT CHEF

Published in 2017 by Hardie Grant Books, an
imprint of Hardie Grant Publishing

Hardie Grant Books (Melbourne)
Building 1, 658 Church Street
Richmond, Victoria 3121
hardiegrantbooks.com.au

Hardie Grant Books (London)
5th & 6th Floors
52–54 Southwark Street
London SE1 1UN
hardiegrantbooks.co.uk

A Cataloguing-in-Publication entry is available
from the catalogue of the National Library of
Australia at www.nla.gov.au
Pana Chocolate, The Recipes
ISBN 978 1 74379 254 4

Publishing Director: Jane Willson
Managing Editor: Marg Bowman
Project Editor: Loran McDougall
Editor: Vanessa Lanaway
Design Manager: Vaughan Mossop
Designer: Andy Warren
Typesetter: Megan Ellis
Photographers: Armelle Habib,
Chris Middleton
Stylist: Vicki Valsamis
Production Manager: Todd Rechner
Production Coordinator: Rebecca Bryson

Colour reproduction by Splitting Image
Colour Studio
Printed and bound in China by 1010 Printing
International Limited